THE MYSTIQUE OF OM

Om is the most sacred mantra in major Indic religions such as Hinduism, Buddhism and Jainism. It symbolises affirmation, benediction and peace. It is also a magical symbol beyond compare.

Using the Vedas, Upanishads, yoga, tantra and several religious texts as his sources, the author describes a plethora of interpretations of this mystical monosyllable which has since time immemorial captivated its worshippers, put yogis into trance, made tantra practitioners ecstatic, and sent its chanters into religious frenzy.

THE MYSTIQUE OF OM

Jayant Burde

New Age Books

ISBN: 81-7822-281-7

First Edition: Delhi, 2007

© 2006 by Jayant Burde

Published by
NEW AGE BOOKS
A-44 Naraina Industrial Area Phase-I
New Delhi-110 028 (INDIA)
Email: nab@vsnl.in
Website: www.newagebooksindia.com

Printed in India
at Shri Jainendra Press
A-45 Naraina Phase-I, New Delhi-110 028

IN MEMORY OF MOTHER (MA)

LEELA

CONTENTS

PREFACE

This book is about Om or Aum which is the most sacred mantra in Hinduism, and which is also revered by Buddhists. It discusses the status of this monosyllable and its several interpretations, including those of its constituents a, u, m.

Om is used at the beginning and at the end of a prayer, and is also a word of solemn invocation. It also serves as a symbol of affirmation, benediction and peace. It is used as a magical symbol which can bestow supernatural powers, and as a vehicle to attain liberation from the cycle of birth and death. However, at the highest level, it is regarded as identical with Brahman, the Ultimate Reality.

There are a number of sources which give us several interpretations of Om : the Vedas and the Upanishads, the Puranas, the *Bhagavad Gita*, yoga and tantra, and hundreds of commentaries. In fact, the religious literature is so vast that the task of extracting the essence of Omkara is really formidable.

I have also included two chapters 15 and 16, which may be said to reflect secular views on Om. Chapter 15 is a brief discussion on the structural or syntactic approach which considers structure as more important than meaning (semantics). Chapter 16 explains how linguists, anthropologists, sociologists and psychologists view about Om.

Since the work is meant for a general reader, I have refrained from using the Devanagari script, Sanskrit verses in the original form, and diacritical marks as far as possible. When such devices appeared to be indispensable, their explanation in simple language is provided. The common reader detests footnotes which I have avoided. However, a few notes on some chapters will be found at the end for those who might be interested in knowing the sources for further reference. The average reader who is averse to 'notes' may ignore them.

The glossary provided at the end of the book will be useful to those who, like me, may tend to forget technical words already introduced earlier. It also contains a few words related to Om which could not be included in the main body of the book, but which you may encounter elsewhere.

I was fortunate in that this work had a smooth sail since I approached the publishers. I am grateful to the staff who completed the administrative formalities without much ado. I particularly appreciate those who were extremely prompt in communicating with me; Mr. Rajiv Jain, Ms Kavita (who has since left NAB), Mr. Om Anand, Ms Jyotsna and Ms Pragya Jain. My special thanks go to those in the editorial department, who have been working, as it were, behind the scenes. Their editing was exhaustive and often merciless which made me feel like a school boy who is being tutored by an unsparing master. However, imagining myself to be in the shoes of the reader was all that was necessary to accept most of their suggestions. Editing may appear a thankless job but I can assure the editors of New Age

Books that they can expect heartfelt gratitude from those authors who are able to rise above hubris.

I am also thankful to Mr. Yashwant Dusane who prepared the DTP version of the manuscript, and designed the figures.

Nashik   JAYANT BURDE

Jan. 2006.

One

OM THAT IS AUM

"The Spirit (*Purusha*) that is the sun, the Spirit, am I Om? The Eternal Brahman."

—Yajurveda (40-17)

"Om let us eat! Om let us drink! Om may the Sun (the shining) god, Varuna, Prajapati and Savitri bring us food here. O lord of food, bring food here, yea, bring it. Om."

—Dogs singing like priests who recite Bahishpavamana hymn (Chhandogya Upanishad 1-12-5).

Om or Aum is the most sacred monosyllable in Hindu tradition, and is also venerated by Buddhists. So sacred is it that according to some traditions, it should not be heard when uttered. In this respect it represents the most sacred objects in primitive societies, which are revered, but are also feared and become taboo. However, you can also see the opposite tendency among the worshippers of Om. The more frequently you use Om, the greater is its benefit because of its mystical power.

Om is used at the beginning and at the end of a prayer. In the latter aspect it resembles Amen and also has connotations of peace. Om is the word of solemn invocation which may be used even on secular occasions.

It is also a symbol of affirmation or benediction, believed to be connected with 'hum' which implies consent. It is used in meditation by ordinary worshippers, yogis and tantriks. It is believed to be a means to achieve liberation (*moksha*) which frees you from the cycle of birth and death. Om is also used as a mantra to have a desired effect or for the fulfilment of one's wishes.

In the theory of sound, it is the primordial syllable from which all words of speech have emanated. When used in conjunction with other mystical symbols, verbal or otherwise, Om is believed to make these symbols more potent. However, at the highest level, Om is Brahman, the Ultimate Reality or Truth. In *advaita* or non-dualism of the Vedantic philosophy, Brahman alone exists, the rest is an illusion (*maya*). Upanishads consider Brahman immortal, eternal, omnipresent, omniscient and Pure Consciousness, as we shall see later.

We do not know when Om entered Indian scriptures. It appears even at the beginning of the Rigveda, the oldest Veda. Of course, it may be that it is a later addition. A similar symbol 'Ahum' is used in the Zoroastrian Gatha with great reverence. It is possible that Om or its variant existed before Aryans entered India.

Om is actually considered to consist of 3½ moras (*matras*), its correct form being Aum, each letter of which is a matra. The last half matra is the silence that follows these letters. More about this later.

According to one theory, the universe emerged from sound vibrations, and Om or Aum is the primordial sound. Om also gave rise to vowels and consonants. The entire acoustic world which emanated from these basic phonemes is called *shabdabrahma* (*shabda* for words, *Brahma* for the creator of the universe). Sound is thus the foundation of everything we see, hear or perceive by other senses. It is also believed that every letter (*matrika*) is a depository of power or *shakti*. This shakti becomes especially intense when certain patterns give rise to the *bija mantras* like em, aim, etc., of which Om is of course, the bija ('seed') par excellence. The bijas are discussed at length later. Om is also called *pranava*. There are a number of definitions of pranava.

(1) It is formed from pra + nu which implies concentration, worshipping or meditating on God with great zeal (*prakarsha*).

(2) Pranava is also interpreted as a combination of prakarsha and nava (new). This means that this worship of God is ever new or novel i.e., it does not become stale or routine.

(3) Scholars cite the maxim "Pranatam avati iti, Om". 'Avati' means protector. The shloka implies that Om is the protector of the one who humbly beseeches help.

(4) The verse-line "Pranamayati iti pranavah" means that Om is that which makes a person bow before the Vedas.

(5) Omkara also means indestructible.

(6) The most important interpretation of Om is that it is Brahman, the Ultimate Reality. This identity has far-reaching consequences. Since Om is Brahman, the question whether Brahman created Om becomes redundant and the assertion that Om created the universe becomes credible.

The symbol Om is not an ordinary combination of the letters of the Sanskrit alphabet. It is believed that the ancient rishis were motivated to use this symbol from the constellation Vrishchika (Scorpio). This newly created symbol is believed to appear like this constellation.

A-U-M

As mentioned earlier Aum consists of 3½ matras. The three letters represent 3 matras while the crescent with a dot supplies the half matra. These matras have been interpreted in several ways. According to one tradition, a human being has three bodies; the outermost is the gross body (*sthula sharira*) which we recognise with our senses in the waking state. Inside the gross body lives the subtle body (*sukshma sharira*) which is the diminutive double of the gross body. This is also called the *linga sharira*. It encompasses mind, energy and wisdom. Its consciousness corresponds to the world of ideas and dreams. Enveloped by the subtle body is the causal body (*karana sharira*) which is without sense organs, but which has the knowledge of sense. It is usually associated with bliss and corresponds to deep sleep.

According to Upanishads each of these bodies is associated with a characteristic consciousness; *vaishvanara, taijasa* and *prajna* respectively. Some scholars recognise a fourth, the innermost body called *mahakarana deha* or sharira. *Maha* means great and mahakarana may be translated as the primal cause. This body has a paradoxical description; minutest, brilliant but omnipresent. Like the individual (*jiva*), God or Ishvara also has four bodies : *virat* (huge), *hiranyagarbha* ('golden womb', Brahman), *maya* and *mulaprakriti*. Of the 3½ matras of AUM, *A* is associated with the sthula sharira, which with proper worship of Om can merge with Ishvara's virat deha. *U* will be similarly absorbed by hiranyagarbha because the letter (U) stands for the jiva's sukshma sharira. *M*, representing our causal body, will merge with Ishvara's maya deha. The remaining half matra representing mahakarana deha will become one with God's mulaprakriti, provided Om is properly worshipped. The worshipper is then in the state called *turiya* and has realised Brahman.

AUM has also been interpreted as the conjunction of earth (A), sky (U) and heaven (M) i.e., *bhuh, bhuvah, svah*. Pranava also means speech (A), mind (U) and life-force (M) i.e., *vak, manas and prana*.

Unbalanced Equation

Vinoba Bhave was a great Gandhian, a social worker, a scholar and a polyglot. He had a very interesting approach to the interpretation of the 'equation':

$$A + U + M = Om$$

According to him, this is not an algebraic equation: Given the values of A, U, M, you do not get Om. For example, A is interpreted as Rigveda, U as Yajurveda and M as Samaveda. But Om is much more than these three Vedas put together. According to him the equation resembles a chemical reaction rather than an algebraic equation. For instance, hydrogen (H) and oxygen (O) when combined under proper conditions give water (H_2O) which has properties quite different from those of its constituents. In modern language, this is tantamount to saying that a Gestalt is something more than the sum of its parts.

Bhave elucidates this fact in a different way. According to him, meditating on A, then on U and then on M is not the same as meditating on the combined AUM. It is only when the three matras are meditated upon as a whole, that you are worshipping the primordial pranava. The half matra, which is often spoken of, automatically follows as an insight in the silence which succeeds the worship of AUM as an entity.

AUM has been interpreted in many ways. The table in Appendix mentions some of the most important interpretations. You should treat this only as a reference chart. Many of the words will be unintelligible to you, but you will come across them in the succeeding chapters. Some of the words can also be found in the Glossary.

Soham

It is believed by some scholars that Om is not a mantra composed or fabricated either by philosophers or by the religious minded. It is a natural sound of the breath.

If you sit at a quiet place preferably with your eyes shut and do not allow external thoughts to intrude your mind, you will feel the rhythm of breathing. If you concentrate on the natural slow inhaling and exhaling you will find the sound 'so' during the process of breathing in and 'ham' when you breath out. The natural sound associated with the normal breathing is 'Soham'. You have been uttering these phonemes ever since you were born. With 'So', you take in the energy while with 'hum' you release the unwanted elements. Pandit Rajamani Tigunait calls Soham 'the universal mantra'.

It is believed that Mother Nature coordinates the pattern of this mantra and every cell of our body participates in uttering this mantra which is in tune with

the natural vibrations of our body. Some scholars call
the regulating force of this mantra *sutratma* (the thread
atma), and also *pranatma* or the 'thread of life'.

Om is embedded in Soham. So-ham means "I am
that" ('So' for that and 'aham' for *I*) which means, "I am
Brahman" according to non-dualism. Those sages who
are in a state of deep samadhi hear this sound, not the
way we hear but as "I am Brahman" semantically, i.e.,
the sage feels that she is Brahman whenever Soham
appears naturally while breathing.

If inhaling and exhaling are separately transliterated
they appear as *sah* and *aham*. But when they merge, the
compound sound becomes Soham. It is believed to
exemplify the grammatical rule viz., an aspirated 'a'
followed by another 'a' becomes 'o'.

In North India there is a religious sect called Natha
Sampradaya. The followers of this sect consider Soham
as an equivalent to Om (o-a-m) which is concealed in
S-o-h-a-m. According to *Goraksha Samhita* (1-41-44),
Soham liberates the yogis and has no parallel.

Both Vedanta and Yoga incorporate Soham in their
practice.

The practice of Soham is believed to relax your body
and mind. The mantra involves the fundamental life-
force, prana. When it is practised under the guidance
of a teacher, it soothes your nerves and produces a sense
of wholeness with the universe. There are undoubtedly
a few problems you face during the practice (*sadhana*).
Unwanted thoughts may intrude your mind or you
may become restless. On the other hand you may
become bored because you find the practice
monotonous in the beginning. But perseverance under
proper guidance is believed to reward you as a

worshipper of God. Moreover, the realisation that you are Brahman i.e., God is within you, gives you infinite peace and courage.

The worship of Soham is the same as the pranava-sadhana or the worship of Om. Since 'Soham' is a natural or an automatic sound it is called 'ajapajapa' or 'ajapa Gayatri'.

In *Siddhacharitra*, a text considered important by Natha Yogis, a 'Soham hamsa' japa to cleanse 'nadis' (carriers of life-energy) is mentioned. Inhale with the left nostril (sah). This is called *puraka*. Retain the breath (*kumbhaka*) pronouncing (in mind) Om twelve times and exhale with the right nostril (ham) which is called *rechaka*.

Another text *Shrigurushishya Vijanana Dipika* makes it clear that Soham, Om, Atman and Brahman are identical. It says:

Om! Know soham hamsa, immortal soham is the japa of hamsa. This knowledge is stored in the form of Atma. Om! Soham is the knowledge Brahman. Om! Soham is nirguna (Unmanifest Reality). Om, Soham is Guru's teaching, it is all Soham-Brahman. Om, Soham is God within me. Om, Soham is Krishna. Om, I see Soham everywhere. Om, it is Shiva and Shakti. Soham is the glory of Pandhari (a town associated with God Vithoba). It is manifest as well unmanifest Krishna. Soham is Brahman. Om, Soham is the four Vedas. Om, Soham is Brahman's word. Soham is the holy revelation. Soham is one in many. Om, Soham is the liberator. Soham is *Bhagvata*. Soham, the bestower of the knowledge of Brahman. Soham is the *Gita*. Om, Soham is the sacred Gayatri. Om, Soham is ajapa complete. Soham makes me ecstatic. It is the knowledge for countless births. It is the meditation for rishis and sages like Shri Gorakshanatha and Dattatreya for accomplishment.

Before we end this chapter a quotation from *Gorakshasamhita* would be instructive. Goraksha Natha was one of the renowned yogis of the Natha sect.

"The prana of the jiva goes out with 'ha' and enters with the sound 'sah'. It thus recites the mantra 'hamsa hamsa'. In one night the jiva makes 21,600 recitations (automatically). This is ajapa Gayatri. It liberates the yogis. Its undertaking frees you from all sins. There is no other knowledge or japa comparable to it. Such knowledge did not exist in the past and will not appear in the future."

Two

THE VEDAS AND BRAHMAN

"By negating all the upadhis through the help of the scriptural
statement 'It is not this, it is not this', realize the oneness of the
individual soul and the Supreme Soul by means of the great
Vedic aphorisms."

Shankara in *Atmabodhah* (Self-knowledge) - 24.

Aryans entered India between 1500 and 100 BCE from
the North-West. They were Indo-European pastoral
nomads who worshipped many gods, composed
beautiful hymns, and performed sacrifices.

The Vedas (from 'vid', to know) were composed
dating from 1500 BCE. There are four Vedas, Rig, Yajur,
Sama and Atharva. The Rigveda is the oldest from which
Yajur and Sama have been derived. The Atharva was
added later.

Vedic Gods

Many gods appear in the Rigveda, most of them
being personifications of the power of nature. The most
important among them were Agni, Indra, Surya and
Varuna.

Agni means fire and its etymology is related to Latin
'ignis'. Hymns were addressed to him at the time of
sacrifice. He consumed the sacrifices and transported
them to other gods in heaven. He was also a god of
mysticism. Since Aryans were warriors, they also had a

warrior god Indra who was also a weather god. Surya
or the Sun was an important god because he supplied
heat and light. He is also identified with gods like
Savitri and Aditya. Varuna (all-embracer) was regarded
as the king of the universe. He was also the guardian of
Rita, the cosmic order.

Soma was a god as well as a plant from which the
hallucinogenic soma juice was extracted. The
exhilarating juice was drunk at the time of sacrifice. He
was regarded as an omnipotent deity who could bestow
riches.

There were also other gods like Aditi (free
unbounded), Prithvi or the earth Yama ('restrained'),
the god of death, Vayu, the wind god.

The Yajurveda contains many hymns borrowed from
the Rig. It contains the rules prescribed for the
performance of sacrifices. The Samaveda, too, contains
verses from the Rig. The verses were tuned to music
and chanted at the time of sacrifices.

The Atharva which belongs to a later period contains
mantras relating to charms, spells and incantations.
Unlike the friendly gods of the first three Vedas, in
Atharva, the gods were a source of terror.

Each Veda had its own priest. Hotri (Hota) recited
the Rigveda, Adhvaryu 'muttered' the formula from the
Yajurveda and Udgatri (Udgata) chanted the mantras
from Samans.

The Vedic society did not know the art of writing
and the Vedas were handed down from one generation
to the next by word of mouth. Hindus revere the Vedas
and believe that they reveal the highest truth.

In addition to many gods there was a mysterious
entity 'One' or 'Brahman'. What's more, the poets saw

one god in many and many gods in one. The lesser gods were identified with the mysterious 'Ekam' (the One) or the Tat Sat (That Being). This is perhaps the stage when Aryans began to believe in the Supreme Being or Ultimate Reality which manifested itself in the form of many gods. The following verses give us some insight into what the Aryans thought about gods.

The one Being, wise call by various names such as Agni, Yama, Matarisshvan (Rigveda 1-164-46).

Agni is That, Aditya is That,
Vayu is That, Chandramas is That,
The bright one is That,
Apah are Those, Prajapati is He.
(Yajurveda 32-1).

In the above 'That' is used in the neuter which is usually applied to the Ultimate Reality.

Consider the following:
Thou art woman, thou art man
Thou art boy, thou art maiden.
Thou art the old man doddering with the staff
Thou existest in all forms (Atharvaveda 10-8-27)

These hymns appear to imagine an omnipresent, omnipotent Being. This Being is identified with the Self. For example:

The Spirit (*Purusha*) that is the sun, the Spirit am I,
Om, the eternal Brahman.
(Yajurveda, Vajasaneyi, 40-17).

While many gods were worshipped making the Aryan society ostensibly polytheistic the above verses show that there was a gradual shift to monism and a belief in the Ultimate Reality called Brahman. The Brahman was also identified with Om and Self (Atman).

Atman is the same as Brahman (Universal soul).

The following verses clearly show that there was early identification of the Reality with Atman.

Men of divine knowledge knew the Spirit that resides with Atman (Self) in the lotus that is the nine-gate (man's) body, enclosed within triple bonds. (Atharvaveda X-8-43).

The ancient sages believed that three gunas (qualities) sattva (light), rajas (force) and tamas (darkness) imprisoned the body-bound soul. When liberated the soul merged with Brahman.

Another example in the Atharvaveda is illuminating:
To him who knows God only as One
Neither second, nor third nor fourth is He termed
Neither fifth nor sixth nor seventh is He called
Neither eighth nor ninth nor tenth is He called

He surveys all that which breathes and does not breathe.

He is the conquering power. He is the One, the One Alone.

In him All Deities become the One Alone.
(Atharvaveda XIII - 4).

(The first verse is repeated after each of the succeeding verses).

These verses are the harbingers of Vedantic monism which is discussed later. The association of Om with Brahman also seems to imply the identity of these entities.

In the following verse the duality of body and spirit is realised:

May my breath reach the eternal sky,
Then let my body end in ashes,

Om, Mind, recall, recall my sphere remember my deeds (Y 40 -15).

In this verse Om merely appears as a sacred word, but when it is compared with other verses, there is no doubt that whatever the original usage of Om (magical word, sacred invocatory prefix) it soon came to be identified with Brahman.

Religion and Dharma

Hinduism has descended from the Vedic 'religion'. Hinduism is not a religion in the sense Islam or Christianity is. It has no founder and no Book. It is usually called a way of life whose cornerstone is *dharma*. The principles of dharma are truth (*satya*), order (*Rita*), consecration (*diksha*), austerity (*tapas*), Brahman (prayer) and ritual (*yajna*). Of these Rita is the most intriguing principle—it is the eternal order which keeps the universe in equilibrium.

Varna

The Vedic society was divided into four classes (varnas). Brahmins belonged to the highest class, their duty being to learn, teach and sacrifice. Below brahmins were kshatriyas or fighters whose duty was to protect society. However, they could also study and sacrifice. Vaishyas were below kshatriyas. They were traders and cattle-breeders. Shudras were the lowest class which supplied labour and served other classes.

The word 'caste' is erroneously employed for varna. Caste roughly means a cohesive group whose common bond is trade and profession.

The Stages of Life

The life of a male belonging to first three varnas consisted of four stages. A male became the full member of society when he underwent an initiation ceremony called *upanayana* after which he became a *brahmacharin*. The two most important aspects of the upanayana were wearing a thread called *yajnopavita* and introducing to him the sacred Gayatri mantra (which is considered in detail later). The brahmacharin went to study under a teacher with whom he stayed and also did chores for him.

After returning from his studies he got married and became a householder. He was obliged to perform certain rituals mentioned in Samhitas and Brahmanas.

When he became old he went to a forest usually with his wife and lived there as a *vanaprastha*. He studied Aranyakas which described symbolic form of worship.

When he became too old, he entered the last stage called *sanyasa*. He renounced all rituals and became a wandering monk. He studied the Upanishads, the concluding part of the Vedas. Upanishads are extremely important for us because, as we shall see, they provide us insights into Brahman, Atman and Om.

The Pantheon

We have already mentioned Vedic gods. Many new gods have been added during the last two thousand years.

Brahma is the creator of the universe and the counterpart of the Vedic Prajapati and Hiranyagarbha.

Vishnu is quite important and he periodically descends on the earth as an incarnation (*avatara*) to destroy the evil. Rama, Krishna are some of the most important avataras.

Shiva is as important as Vishnu and may be called the successor of the Vedic Rudra. He is at once the god of creation and destruction. He has matted hair through which the sacred river Ganges flows. We will meet him often in connection with Om.

Brahma the creator, Vishnu the preserver and Shiva the destroyer form a *trimurti* or trinity widely worshipped all over India.

Ganesha is the elephant-headed son of Shiva and Parvati. He is called the remover of obstacles. (*Vighnaharta*)

In chapter 6, we shall discuss Ganesha in connection with pranava.

There are also many goddesses such as Lakshmi, Vishnu's wife. Sarasvati, Brahma's consort and Parvati, Shiva's spouse. There is also Mother goddess who symbolises not only femininity but Shakti (power.) Shakti has great importance in tantra which we shall study in a later chapter.

Darshana

The word *darshana* is a poor equivalent of 'philosophy'. It means direct vision. Unlike the Western concept Indian philosophy connotes a practical aspect. While the theoretical frame does exist, philosophy is to be experienced. More often than not, it is a search for the Ultimate Reality.

There are six traditional 'schools' which claim allegiance to the Vedas. They are Nyaya, Vaisheshika, Sankhya, Yoga, Mimamsa and Vedanta.

Nyaya or analysis believes in individual soul and posits that a person is liberated when he attains valid knowledge or *tattvajnana* of the soul. It regards God as the creator of the universe out of atoms, space, time, mind and soul, all of which are eternal. Vaisheshika is similar to Nyaya but treats uniqueness as a category. It emphasises the importance of dharma for achieving the highest goal in life.

Sankhya is a dualistic philosophy and recognises two categories; Purusha, the conscious principle and Prakriti the unconscious principle. These two interact to produce the universe. Since Purusha (Father) and Prakriti (Mother) formed a self-sufficient complex, God was not recognised earlier by Sankhya philosophers. However, under the influence of monism and theism, the existence of God was later incorporated. The philosophy asks you to realise that Purusha (Self) is different from senses. The former is eternal. When you begin to understand the true nature of the self, you are liberated.

Yoga is another system which is based on the possibility of expanding the individual's consciousness so that it merges with the universal consciousness. The word yoga comes from the root 'yuj' which means to unite. Patanjali Yoga Sutra (2nd century CE) is one of the most important texts in Yoga.

Mimamsa (enquiry) is the fifth school which is also called Purva Mimamsa. It treats human life as a grand ritual. The sixth system is Vedanta which is also called Uttara Mimamsa. It means the end of the Vedas, and its philosophy reflects the teachings of Upanishads and Vyasa's *Brahma Sutras*.

From our point of view Yoga, Mimamsa and Vedanta are of utmost importance. We discuss below Mimamsa and Vedanta while Yoga is detailed in a separate chapter.

Mimamsa and the Theory of Sound

Mimamsa was founded by Jaimini (ca 200 BCE) whose *Mimamsa Sutra* is an important text. Shabara, Kumarila and Prabhakara (7th century) also made great contributions to this school.

Mimamsa elaborates a method to interpret the Vedas. Mandan Mishra's *Mimamsa Anukramanika* is a text which elucidates this interpretative technique. Mimamsa also provides a rationale for ritual. According to it the performance of ritual is man's highest dharma.

For us, however, the theory of sound propounded by Mimamsa is more important. Mimamsa explains the efficacy of rituals and mantras. By mantras its adherents mean the Vedic verses.

According to Mimamsa, though the perception of sound appears momentary sound, as such it is eternal. Literally *vak* in Sanskrit means sound or speech but for Mimamsa it has a wider connotation—it includes thought as well as the consequent expression. This means that vak shakti or the power of the sound precedes the actual utterance. Mimamsa analyses vak shakti at length and finds four levels called *vaikhari, madhyama, pashyanti* and *para*.

Vaikhari represents the lowest level or the last temporal stage where sound appears in the audible form. At the higher level vak is at the madhyama (middle) stage. Here, the power has already formed a concrete thought pattern about to be expressed audibly. The next higher stage is called pashyanti ('one who sees') which is the unmanifest shakti of vak. It is often referred to as a universal language or the language of silence which is the ultimate source of speech as well as language. This can also be identified with the Ultimate Reality or Supreme Consciousness or Brahman of Vedanta.

The para vak is the highest stage—it is the primordial, eternal sound identified once again with the highest

Reality. However, the difference between pashyanti and para vak is not very clear since both represent Brahman. We may interpret this difference in two ways. (1) Para vak is the dormant pashyanti because in pashyanti, the supreme consciousness 'sees the entire universe in its primeval desire.'[1] (2) We may subscribe to the view that originally there was the primordial sound Om, from which the universe has been created.

In any case, we may say that the vak shakti flows from para to pashyanti to madhyama and thence to vaikhari where it becomes audible.

According to Mimamsa the sound manifestation has two inseparable parts, *shabda* (audible sound) and *artha* or the object (form). This thought leads to an interesting philosophy. The sound patterns constitute mantras while the forms are deities. We can say, therefore, that every acoustic complex is a duo consisting of a deity and the corresponding mantra. Mimamsa postulates that a sound pattern may convert itself into the corresponding deity, and conversely a deity may dematerialise into its acoustic counterpart viz., mantra. Mimamsa however explains that the different deities which correspond to different sound patterns ultimately indicate various manifestations of the same Ultimate Reality.

Mimamsa believes that cosmic powers can be harnessed by using the right sound patterns or mantras through the manipulation of physical objects in ritual.

This philosophy leads to two interpretations. One, the use of physical objects implies that divinity is omnipresent, not confined to particular portion of the physical world. These thoughts lead to Vedanta or Uttara Mimamsa. Second, the sound patterns (mantras) representing different gods are nothing but the manifestations of the primordial sound - Om or pranava.

Vedanta

Vedanta is the most important darshana for us, because it unifies Atman (Self), Brahman, the Ultimate Reality and pranava or Om.

There are different schools of Vedanta founded by Shankara, Ramanuja, Madhva, Vallabha and Nimbarka. However, Shankara's advaitism or non-dualism has influenced Hindus, and recently Indian intellectuals as no other school has.

The important Vedantic schools other than monism are qualified monism and dualism. Unlike other darshanas like Nyaya and Sankhya, all schools of Vedanta hold that there is God the Supreme Consciousness and the Ultimate Reality. Without the principle of consciousness one cannot imagine creation.

The concept of Self in Shankara's monism (advaita) is all-pervading consciousness. It is beyond the pale of space, time and causation. While the Self is within the body, it is also outside the body. It is a witness to the various states of man who is born, has experiences and ultimately dies. When a person says he has a body, mind or brain and that he can rationally think, he is not aware that his perception comes from Atman (Self). The average person, therefore, does not know that he is Atman because Atman cannot be felt by mere senses.

To borrow a metaphor from Vedantins, Atman is like an ocean of bliss and consciousness and the individuals are mere waves in the ocean.

Atman is thus eternal and indestructible which an ordinary person cannot fathom.

Brahman according to Shankara is the ultimate Truth. Brahman is all-pervading and self-illumined conscio- usness. Everything that is manifest or unmanifest i.e., everything that exists is Brahman. Without Brahman there is nothing. If we perceive diverse entities, it is merely on account of our ignorance or *avidya*. This is also called *maya* or cosmic illusion.

Atman and Brahman are one in reality. There may be individual souls, but their collective existence is Brahman. Brahman is eternal and is compared with the self-effulgent sun that radiates knowledge, bliss and consciousness.

In truth those who believe in extreme monism do not speak of liberation because the self (Atman) and the Ultimate Reality (Brahman) are the same. It is true that most writers while describing advaita speak of liberation from bondage, but that should be interpreted as the individual's ability to lift the veil of maya and see the truth : the truth that Atman is Brahman. This truth has, however, always existed.

If there is only Brahman, how do we explain the universe and multiplicity? Monists posit that the truth is veiled by maya. They borrow from the Rigveda according to which Indra or Reality assumes a plethora of forms.

Maya is the power of Brahman which, too, is eternal but unconscious. From the viewpoint of individuals it is ignorance or avidya. Inasmuch as it projects the universe, it may be said to be positive while its property to conceal Brahman displays its negative nature. Maya is called real as well as unreal because from the viewpoint of the universe it is real while as to Brahman it is unreal.

What is important for the seeker of truth is that maya can be unveiled through proper understanding.

You can see maya from different angles. Brahman along with its maya is called Ishvara or Saguna Brahman. The individual self associated with maya through ignorance is called *jivatman. Upadhi* is the term used to indicate the apparent difference between Atman and Brahman conditioned by maya.

Rajamani Tigunait in his *Seven Systems of Indian Philosophy* aptly points out "Brahman associated with maya is the material cause of the universe, and Brahman unassociated with maya is the efficient cause of the universe."

According to a Vedantic view the entire physical world results from the vibration of the life force (*prana*) which is not different form maya. The world includes not only living and nonliving objects but also gravitational, magnetic and other forces. According to the Veda, prana existed before the universe, Paradoxical though it may sound there was neither existence nor non-existence. There was no space and time. Only the Supreme Being "was breathing without breath." From this Brahman and maya-prana emerged the universe. You will see that the very conception of Brahman requires the use of paradoxes and oxymorons. For example, it is contented that Brahman can only be described as "neti neti". (It is not this, it is not this). Brihadaranyaka Upanishad (2-3-5).

Vedanta recognises five koshas or sheaths of non-self. They are (1) the gross physical sheath which we call body (*annamayakosha*) which is the outermost cover. (2) The next is the energy sheath (*pranamayakosha*) which is finer than the first and impels the body to action. (3)

Under the energy sheath is the sheath of mind (*manomayakosha*). The fourth sheath is the sheath of intelligence (*vijnanamayakosha*). Buddhi reflects Pure Intelligence. This reflection of Supreme Consciousness in Buddhi is called jiva or the individual soul. Through ignorance the upadhi of jivahood is imposed on Atman. The last sheath is the sheath of bliss (*anandamayakosha*) which is still finer. However, it is a mere reflection of the Supreme Bliss which is captured by Prakriti. This sheath is responsible for mundane bliss. However, its full manifestation is believed to be experienced in deep sleep.

Beneath these sheaths is Atman or Self which in reality is not fettered, but the koshas are dependant on it. It provides intelligence to the intellect, vitality to prana and also sustenance to the body.

Realisation

As we mentioned earlier, in pure monism there is no liberation because Atman is Brahman. What comes between us and Brahman is avidya or ignorance which is maya in terms of the power of Brahman. Realisation that we are not different from the Ultimate reality comes through spiritual practice (*sadhana*). Vedanta prescribes three stages; s*hravana, manana* and *nididhyasana*. Shravana includes studying scriptures and learning from enlightened teachers, the difference between physical objects and Self. *Manana* involves contemplation, introspection, meditation and analysis of the basic conceptions of advaita. Nididhyasana means the actual application of advaitism in practice. It is not enough to realise the identity of Atman and Brahman and differentiate them from the body-mind complex. Our life-style should be fully involved with the concept so that we feel the actual state of affairs. Vedanta is called *jnanayoga* because it has a large component of jnana which should be interpreted as true understanding.

There are four stages of self-realisation which reflect a gradual progress towards understanding and feeling the full import of monism. They are based on the four *maha vakyas* or great statements.

1. Brahman alone is real and the universe is unreal.
2. There is only one Brahman without the second.
3. I am Brahman.
4. The entire universe is Brahman.

We have already mentioned that contemplation and meditation are essential constituents of the Vedantic method of Self-realisation.

In Vedanta, contemplation implies discriminating between the real and the unreal so that we can feel the Ultimate Reality. Om or pranava, the primordial sound is used as a primary object of contemplation.

Patanjali's yoga (*rajayoga*) which will be described in detail later has a similar approach. It emphasises the contemplation on the meaning. It explicitly asserts that Om is the Supreme Reality. Rajayoga and Vedanta both prescribe the same method of repeating Om while breathing.

As mentioned earlier Vedanta treats Om as composite of three phonemes A-U-M which denote waking, dreaming and deep sleep. The fourth state is silence called *turiya*. This may be compared with samadhi of rajayoga when the sadhaka attains Brahman or feels that he is Brahman.

The Vedanta teacher expects you to possess a few prerequisites before you start towards self-realisation. You must learn to calm your mind, purify your emotions, have complete control over the senses. What's more, you must be prepared to be guided by your teacher. The most important motivation you have to possess is a thirst for Realisation through the path of knowledge.

Three

UPANISHADS I

Aitareya, Katha, Taittiriya

"Om Peace, Peace, Peace."
—The end of the invocation appearing in many Upanishads.

We have mentioned earlier that the forest-dwellers who were at the third stage of life, studied Aranyakas. The Upanishads with a few exceptions form the concluding portions of Aranyakas. They are also called Vedanta ('anta' for end) though Vedanta as a philosophy was developed by Vyasa, Gaudapada, Shankara and others.

Etymologically the word Upanishad can be translated as the wisdom learnt from a competent teacher, which completely loosens and destroys the student's attachment to the relative world.

Upanishads teach us the knowledge of Brahman, the Ultimate Reality which is omniscient, omnipresent and is beyond the pairs of opposites, diseases, the relative world and death. There are about 108 surviving Upanishads of which a dozen are major texts. Most Upanishads discuss Om and equate it with Brahman. We shall briefly discuss seven Upanishads viz., Aitareya, Taittiriya, Shvetashvatara, Chhandogya, Mandukya, Katha, Maitrayani and Prashna.

Aitareyopanishad

This Upanishad belongs to the Rigveda and is part of the Aitareyaranyaka and is attributed to Mahidasa Aitareya. This is a short Upanishad which teaches the essence of Brahmavidya (knowledge of Brahman). Its principles may be summarised as below. These tenets are also called Atmavidya.

1. The eternal Atman alone is the substance of the universe
2. Though we see his creations, in reality everything is Atman.
3. Atman is pure consciousness (prajnana) and the essential Self of man.
4. Prajnana or Atman has become everything from Indra, Prajapati, the earth, sun, down to the lowest animate and inanimate objects.
5. A person who has deep and direct realization of peerless Atman attains immortality. This is Brahmavidya.

Atman, here, should be interpreted as Brahman.

The Upanishad does not discuss Om explicitly, but the association of Om, with peace, appearing in the introductory *shantipatha* or 'peace invocation' is significant. Shantipathas also appear in other Upanishads of the Rigveda origin. These Upanishads also end with the 'shantipatha'. The shantipatha in this Upanishad may be translated as follows :

Om ! May my speech rest on mind; may my mind be in speech. O self-manifest Brahman, reveal yourself to me. May your mind and speech help me to grasp the truth that the Vedas teach. May my Vedic lore not forsake me. By that (spiritual) learning, I join day and night. I shall think and speak the truth. May that protect me. May that protect the teacher.

Om peace, peace, peace.

The import of the last line, Om shantih, shantih, shantih, is discussed later in this chapter.

Kathopanishad

This Upanishad is believed to be part of the Brahmana of the Katha Shakha of the Krishna Yajurveda.

This is the story of Nachiketas, son of Vajashravasa who sacrificed all his wealth expecting to get divine boons in return. When the son saw the cows being taken for sacrifice, he asked his father "To whom will you give me?" When he repeated the question three times the exasperated father said "I give you to Death."

The obedient Nachiketas goes to the house of Yama, the god of death. In the absence of the host he stays there for three days without taking any food. Yama, when he returns home, is pained at the guest having stayed at his house without food.

He allows Nachiketas to ask for three boons (corresponding to three nights' stay). Nachiketas replies "Let me return alive to my father." Yama readily grants this boon. 'Ask for a second boon', he says. Nachiketas replies 'Instruct me how my good deeds may not be destroyed'. Yama then teaches him the secrets of a sacrifice, now called Nachiketa Agni, which fulfills his wish. Yama then asks him, what he wants for the third boon?

The third boon, Nachiketas asks is that Yama should tell him how to conquer death? Yama is shocked and offers him other alluring boons which Nachiketas refuses. The Upanishad tells us that Yama ultimately yields and explains to him the mode of conquering death.

Nachiketas follows his "instructions and realises Brahman."

The knowledge Yama imparts to Nachiketas is, in fact, repetition of the Nachiketa yajna, and something more. This includes the knowledge of Om, Atman and Brahman.

In (2-15) Yama mentions Om.

'The goal', he says, which all Vedas proclaim and which all penances declare, and which impels one to Brahmacharya (celibacy)—I tell it to you in nutshell, it is Om.

In the next stanza he says that the syllable Om is Brahman and also the highest. Having known Om one gets whatever one desires.

What Yama means is that Om is *saguna Brahman* (Ishvara or Personal God), and its true knowledge takes you to *nirguna Brahman*, the Brahman without gunas, the Ultimate Reality.

Yama then adds that this support (Om) is the best available means to realise the Supreme Being. Those who fully realise the significance of Om are worshipped in the world of Brahman.

Yama then goes on to explain how Atman differs from the body and is indestructible and eternal and hence it is through Atman one can realise Brahman, the Ultimate Reality.

The Upanishad concludes by observing that Nachiketas having been instructed by Yama the whole process, which the poet calls yoga, became free from all impurities and death, and attained Brahman. Those who follow these instructions and understand the inner self too, will realise Brahman.

There is also a shantipatha at the beginning and in the end which is quite illuminating, and may be mentioned here.

Om saha navavatu/Sahanau bhunaktu/Sahaviryam
Karavavahai/ Tejasvinavadhimastu/Ma vidvisha-
vahai// Om Shantih/Shantih/Shantih//

Om! May He (Brahman) protect us (preceptor and
the disciple). May he nourish us both. May we both
work together with great energy. May our learning be
thorough and yield fruits. May we never hate each other.
Om shantih shantih shantih.

Shantih means peace, its invocation thrice is believed
to ward off three types of hurdles to study viz.: bodily
(adhyatmika), terrestrial (adhibhautika) and heavenly
(adhidaivika).

Taittiriyopanishad

Etymologically, the Taittiriya recension of the
Yajurveda is related to 'tittiri' or partridges of a story
narrated in the *Mahabharata*. The Upanishad is part of
Taittiriya Aranyaka. It seems to have influenced
Shankaracharya immensely. Apart from Brahman,
pranava, meditation etc., it also discusses phonetics.
The Upanishad consists of three chapters, (1) Shiksha—
valli (2) Ananda–valli, and (3) Bhrigu–valli. These are
subdivided into lessons (Anuvakas).

In the very first lesson of chapter one, the composer
connects Om, which is Brahman, with peace. The lesson
ends with "Om shantih shantih shantih" or Om, peace
peace, peace. As mentioned earlier the word peace is
uttered thrice ostensibly to ward off internal, external
and heavenly causes of trouble - adhyatmika,
adhidaivika and adhibhautika *dukkha* (misery).

Lesson 4 of chapter 1 is quite interesting from our
viewpoint. According to it, He who is the *rishabha*
(literally bull, meaning the most excellent.) in the hymns
of the Vedas, who has many forms, who has sprung up

in splendour from the sacred hymns; may he cheer me with intellectual process. O God, let me have the immortal Revelation. May I have sweet speech which will be agreeable. May I listen abundantly so that I may learn. You are the sheath of the Supreme Being. I beseech you to preserve My learning.

Advaitism interprets rishabha as Om which is the symbol of Brahman. From the theistic point of view, Om is the object of meditation which was discovered by Prajapati for the benefit of the world. The dualist may treat Om as a mere device to realise Brahman.

There is thus a dilemma for monists especially because Om is also referred to as the cover, which contradicts the conception of one and only one Brahman. This apparent contradiction would also strengthen the arguments of the dualists. However, the monists usually explain the apparent dualism through the doctrine of maya. It can also be argued that the cover is a mere metaphor and at the highest level the vehicle through which Brahman is worshipped is not different from Brahman itself.

In the same lesson the poet describes how the worshipper through oblations expects realization of Brahman. The oblations are believed to destroy the past sins. One of his pleas is "In that Self of Yours with a thousand branches may I cleanse myself of all sins." Achyutakrishnananda believes that 'thousand branches' refers to various texts of the Veda, which are merely expressions of pranava or Om.[1]

Lesson 5 of the same chapter tells us how Om, Brahman Atman and vyahritis are inseparably connected.

It says that bhuh, bhuvah suvah are great mystical utterances. In addition to these there is a fourth one.

This is Mahah, which is Brahman as well as Atman. This was discovered by Mahachamasya.

All other gods are the limbs of Brahman. Bhuh stands for this world, the sacred verses Riks and the air we breathe in (*pranah*). Bhuvah is the space between the earth and the heaven. It also indicates the Saman chants and the air we breathe out (*apanah*). Suvah is the heaven, the sun, the sacrificial formulae of the Yajurveda. It also means the vital air which sustains life when the respiration is arrested (*vyanhah*). Mahah is the sun, moon and also Brahman or Om. It also means food. Through the sun all worlds, through the moon all lights and through Brahman all the Vedas and through food all animate beings are 'magnified' and strengthened. These are the four vyahritis forming a quartet. He who meditates on them knows Brahman and to him all gods pay homage. The identification of Om with Brahman is explicit in this verse.

Actually, there are seven vyahritis : *janah, tapah* and *satya* in addition to the four mentioned here. They represent the seven upper worlds. It is interesting to know that mahah is derived from a root which means 'great or grow without limit'. Brahman also has the same root. Mahah thus appears to be on par with Brahman in relation to Atman for the purpose of meditation. The lesson suggests that those who want to attain Brahman should meditate on Atman as if it were mahah.

Lesson 8, of the same chapter is equally forthright about the identity of Om.

One should contemplate : Om is Brahman. The entire universe perceived or imagined is Om. It is known to all that Om is the term of compliance. Those priests who officiate at the sacrifice command their assistant as follows: O Agnidhra, let Devas (gods) know that the oblation is about to be offered. Starting with Om, Udgatri (Udgata) priests start chanting the Samans. Uttering Om Som, the Hotri (Hota) priests recite the invocations. The Adhavaryu responds to Hotri by uttering Om. Brahma then utters Om which impels the performing priest to begin the act of sacrifice. The sacrificer then authorises to offer the oblation uttering Om. A brahmana proceeds to recite the Veda after he says Om. Surely, he attains Brahman.

The verse asks one to meditate on Om which is the acoustic manifestation of Brahman. Om is also prefixed to almost every act or utterance.

According to Swami Vivekanada "Symbol is the manifestor of the thing signified and if the thing signified is already in existence, and if by experience we know that the symbol has expressed that thing many times, then we are sure that there is a real relation between them. The idea of God is connected with hundreds of words and each one stands as a symbol for God. But there must be a generalisation among all these words, some substratum, some common ground of all these symbols; and that which is the common symbol will be the best and really represent them all. Om is such a sound, the basis of all sounds. The first letter 'a' is the root sound the key pronounced without touching any part of the tongue or palate; 'm' represents the last sound in the series being produced by the closed lips, and the 'u' rolls from the very root to the end of the sounding board of the mouth. Thus Om represents the whole phenomena of sound-producing. As such it must be the natural symbol. The matrix of all the various sounds. It denotes the whole range and possibility of all the words that can be made."[2]

Om, since it prevades the whole universe, is no other than Brahman.

Four

UPANISHADS II

Shvetashvatara, Chhandogya

With Upanishads as your bow and constant upasana as the arrow, with Om as the bow and Atma as your arrow, penetrate (attain) the immortal Brahman.

—Mundakopanishad (2-3-4)

Shvetashvatara

This small Upanishad consisting of 113 mantras belongs to the Krishnayajurveda. Shvetashvatara is believed to be an honorific title conferred upon a great rishi who taught this Upanishad to his disciples. The title means "one who has controlled himself" ('shveta' for pure and 'ashva' for indriyas or senses).

The Upanishad is eclectic and borrows from monism (advaita), dualism (dvaita), qualified non-dualism (Vishishta advaita) schools of Vedanta. One also finds the influence of the Sankhya and Yoga philosophy.

It treats Om as Brahman but the monosyllable is commented upon in various chapters unlike some other Upanishads such as Prashna.

Before we deal with the philosophy relating to pranava it would be worthwhile to mention the renowned first stanza of the peace invocation.

Om, everything that is invisible is filled by Brahman, everything that is visible is permeated by Brahman. The entire universe originated from the whole Brahman. Though the whole universe came out of Brahman, Brahman is still full.

This explains the aspect of Brahman which is inexhaustible.

In (1-13) the rishi explains that Atman is ever-existent in you but is latent. Till the fire-stick is not ignited by percussion, fire is not visible in its cause. The essence of fire nevertheless exists in the stick. Atman is similar to the dormant fire. When you meditate on pranava, Atman is perceived in the body. The meditation on Om is thus the cause of spiritual fire which helps you realise Atman.

In the next couplet (1-14) a metaphor referring to the churning device is used. Your body is the lower wooden piece of the device and Om or pranava is the upper piece. Your meditation resembles the act of churning which results in your realising God. Pranava is thus a vehicle used to reach God.

It is interesting to note that churning is often compared with learning in which the upper piece is the teacher and the disciple forms the lower piece.

The Upanishad borrows from the yoga science in (2-8). The rishi asks you to place the body in a straight posture. The chest, throat and head must be held erect. You should draw the senses and mind into the heart as the yogi checks the outgoing tendencies by practising pratyahara. If you know the meaning of Om or pranava, you will be able to cross all the obstacles or the fearful currents which might take the ignorant to the cycle of birth and death. You will be able to cross the current with the help of the 'raft or Brahman'—which is nothing but the Taraka—Brahman or Pranava. The japa of Om will help you realize Brahman.

In chapter (3-6) the rishi appeals to God to protect him and his disciples.

O revealer of the Vedic truth, condescend to make your arrow propitious.

The mystic monosyllable Om refers to the arrow. Pranava also means the impersonal (nirguna) and personal (saguna) Brahman.

The rishi appeals to God not to use the arrow for destruction of the universe which is the manifest form of Brahman itself.

'Arrow' also refers to a Vedic aphorism (maha vakya) or taraka (protection) mantra i.e., Om which is the essence of the Vedas. It is believed that God uses these weapons to destroy ignorance. It is hoped that by uttering Om repeatedly Brahman will be realised.

Chhandogya

According to Shankaracharya, Chhandoga is the singer of Samans. 'Chhando sama gayati iti chhandogah'. Hence Chhandogya is what belongs to the followers of the Samaveda. The Chhandogya Upanishad is believed to form four-fifths of a Chhandogya Brahmana.

This Upanishad has a peace invocation in the beginning and at the end of the treatise. It says :

Om! Let my limbs, speech, prana (vital force), eyes, ears, vitality and all the senses grow from strength to strength. All existence is Brahman. May Brahman not deny me. Let there be no denial (which implies Brahman encompasses all). Let there be no denial at least from me (since I know Brahman is not different from me). May the virtues that are proclaimed in the Upanishad be in me. I am devoted to Atman. May these virtues reside in me.

Om Peace! Peace! Peace!

The first verse of the section one, chapter one, asserts that one should meditate on Om, the Udgitha, because one sings Udgitha beginning with Om. Om actually means the Supreme Being, but can also mean the symbol which when repeated, pleases Him.

Samans are divided into five or seven parts. One of the parts is Udgitha which is sung by the Udgathri priest. He starts singing by intoning Om. Udgitha is a part of the Saman representing the Soma sacrifice. The Udgitha Om is that Om which is sung by the concerned priest Udgathri. The Upanishad recognises the difficulty experienced by the worshipper to meditate on mere Om. Initially, therefore, meditation is a part of the sacrifice, the stage of pure meditation appears at the second step.

According to the second verse, the essence of all the beings is the earth, the essence of the earth is water, the essence of water is vegetation, the essence of vegetation is man whose essence is speech. The essence of speech is Rik. The essence of Rik is Saman. The essence of Saman is Udgitha. Since Om encompasses all sounds, it is the essence of all essences. Om is the Supreme Self.

Speech is Rik and Prana is Saman. The syllable Om is Udgitha. Speech and Prana which are the source of Rik together form a couple. (1-1-3). This couple is joined in the syllable Om.

A person who meditates on Om as Udgitha knowing it as the fulfiller of the wishes (1-1-7) realises all his desirable ends.

Om also means assent which leads to prosperity. One who meditates on Om as Udgitha acquires increased prosperity.

The worship of Om is the worship of Brahman itself which leads to the three fold knowledge. With Om, one causes to listen. With Om one recites and with Om, one sings alone. It is on account of the greatness of this syllable that the Vedic rites can be performed. (1-1-9)

The first section concludes by mentioning the distinction between two worshippers, one who merely utters Om and one who utters it with knowledge (meaning), faith and meditation. The latter's worship is definitely more effective. Thus mere ritual is not enough, the full knowledge of Om is necessary to obtain the maximum benefit.

The second section, chapter 1 of the Upanishad extols the virtues of prana and says that one who meditates on the Udgitha as the syllable Om looking upon it as prana, becomes the singer and the procurer of the desired objects. The poet calls this, the meditation with reference to the body.

In section three, meditation on Udgitha with reference to gods is prescribed. One should meditate on the sun as Udgitha. The sun dispels the darkness and fear and is also responsible for supplying heat for crops.

We are also exhorted to meditate on the syllables of Udgitha. The syllables are interpreted in different ways. For example, *ut* represents heaven, *gi* the sky and *tha* the earth, *Ut* is heaven the Samaveda, *gi* the Yajus, and *tha* is Rig.

Verses (1-4-1) to (1-4-5) explain the greatness of Om. Once the gods afraid of Death, took refuge in three Vedas. Death, however, was smarter and could see them just as a fisherman would see a fish in water. The gods then entered the svara (Om). Having meditated on Om the gods became fearless and immortal. One who worships this syllable with awareness, merges with it. He becomes immortal as if Om were nectar.

According to (1-5-1), Udgitha is the same as pranava. Hence the sun is Udgitha as well as pranava, for it is believed that the sun moves along pronouncing Om.

Verse (1-5-3) advises us to meditate on the main prana in mouth, for prana moves along reciting Om. This Om is, as it were, permission of the vital breath.

Since pranava and Udgitha are identical, one who inadvertently makes mistakes in Udgitha chanting even from the seat of Hota priest is forgiven. (1-5-5)

Brahman is sometimes referred to as akasha (which usually means sky or ether). In (1-9-2) the poet asserts that Udgitha (Om) is progressively higher and higher and endless. He who meditates with this knowledge on progressively higher and better Udgitha obtains progressively higher and better lives, and reaches higher and higher worlds. The verse implies that the meditation on Om progressively takes the worship higher and higher towards Akasha which is Brahman. Here Om is a vehicle to reach Brahman because it symbolises the Supreme Reality.

The Upanishad initially deals with the worship of Samaveda in which Om occurs as Udgitha. Later the text considers Sama-bhakti and the attendant rites as subsidiary and the meditation of pranava or Om as Brahman is considered vital. Verses (2-23-2) and (2-23-3) are also interesting. They show that the bhakta has reached a higher stage.

According to these verses, Prajapati (Brahman) brooded on the words which led to the creation of the three Vedas. When he contemplated on them, syllables bhuh, bhuvah, svah issued. When he continued to meditate on their essence, the syllable Om (Brahman itself) issued forth. Just as all the parts of a leaf are covered by its ribs, all words are permeated by Om— Om is verily all this. Omkara and Paramatman are the same and the universe is only its modification.

Verse (2-23-1) tells us that there are three branches of religious duties. Sacrifice, study and gifts constitute the first duty, austerity is the second. The third duty pertains to the celibate student who lives in his guru's house for life, mortifying his body. Such a student is called Naisthika Brahmacharin unlike the regular students. All these people who perform their duties, attain meritorious worlds. But one who is established firmly in Brahman or Om, attains immortality.

(8-6-4) and (8-6-5) mention the state of the one who is about to die. When such a person is extremely debilitated, those around him ask him, whether he can recognise them. So long as he has not left the body, he may be able to identify them. However, when he departs he may travel upwards through the appropriate sun rays provided he knows the right method viz., meditating on Om. In a short time such a person reaches the sun. The sun is the door to the world of Brahman. Thus the ignorants who do not know the correct method of meditating on Om are shut out from this abode.

The discussion on this Upanishad will not be complete if we omit the interesting section twelve from chapter 1.

Many things are associated with Udgitha including the sun, akasha (Brahman) and Om. This section describes how dogs perceive Udgitha. Once Dalbhya Baka, also called Maitreya Glava, went out of the village to study the Vedas. He saw a white dog who was surrounded by other dogs. The dogs begged the white dog to obtain food for them for they were hungry. The white dog asked them to come there the next morning. Dalbhya Baka kept a watch for them there. The chosen time morning was appropriate because the sun, the supplier of food would be in front of them.

The dogs gathered at the appointed time. They behaved as the priests Ardhvayu Prastotri, Udgathri Pratihartri and the Yajamana normally behave on the last day of the Soma sacrifice when the Soma juice is extracted. The singing priests recite Bahishpavamana hymn. The singing priests move along clasping one another's hand. The dogs acted as if they were singers, after which they sat down and began to pronounce the sacred word Om in the following way.

'Om let us eat! Om let us drink! Om may the sun (the shining) god, Varuna (who causes rains), Prajapati (who protects the people) and Savitri bring us food here. O Lord of food (sun) bring here, yea bring it, Om.'

This passage which has been quoted at the beginning of the book is interesting. It has been interpreted charitably according to which the white dog is in fact a deity or sage who is pleased with Dalbhya's studies with a view to helping him.

It can also be interpreted satirically in which the sacred Om is misused by dogs who try to ape the priests.

Chapter three of the Upanishad describes the meditation on the result of the sacrifice. The sun stands for the result of one's own actions and epitomises the highest ends of the worshippers viz., gradual liberation.

The chapter invokes Om and says that the yonder sun is indeed the honey of the gods. Of this honey heaven is the crossbeam. The sky is the honeycomb and the (water particles in the) rays are the eggs.

The sun is compared with honey because like honey it pleases gods. The heaven is compared with the beam from which the honeycomb hangs. The honeycomb is compared with the dome-like sky. Rays stand for the water particles drawn and held by them. They exist in the hive and resemble the eggs of the bee. After describing various sections or 'rays', it says that the upper rays are the honey cells. The sacred teachings (instructions known to a few priests as well as meditators) are the bees. Brahman (pranava or Om) is the flower. Those waters which arise from the meditation of the pranava are the nectar.

According to (3-5-2) it is these secret teachings which 'press' the pranava. The activated pranava (Om) issues forth as juice, fame, splendor of limbs, alertness of the senses, virility and food for eating.

According to Swami Swahananada, Om is also called Adi (the first) in Chhandogya Upanishad. In (2-8-1) and (2-8-2) the Upanishad exhorts us to meditate on the sevenfold Saman as speech. Whatever in speech is 'hum' that is the syllable 'him'; whatever is 'pra' that is Prastava; whatever is 'a', that is Adi (the first or Om); whatever is 'ut' that is Udgitha' whatever is 'prati' that is Pratihara; whatever is 'upa' that is Upadrava and whatever is 'ni' is Nidhana. It may be mentioned here that the Saman is divided into five or seven parts. The five-fold division is Himkara, Prastava, Udgitha, Pratihara and Nidhana. The seven divisions are Himkara, Prastava, Adi, Udgitha, Pratihara, Upadrava and Nidhana.

It is necessary to remember that Udgitha is a division of the Samaveda, but can also mean Om or akasha, depending on the context.

Five

UPANISHADS III

Mandukya, Prashna, Maitrayani

"Just as dream and magic are perceived to be unreal, or as a city in the sky, so also is this entire universe known to be unreal from the Upanishads by the wise."

—Gaudapada in *Karika* (2-31)

Mandukya

Mandukya Upanishad is certainly one of the most important texts relating to Om. The name is derived from the sage Manduka, and it belongs to the Atharvaveda. However, since the Mandukya verses are terse, one usually reads it with commentaries. In this chapter we shall use Gaudapada's *Karika* (expository treatment) for elucidation. Gaudapada was a renowned scholar, a monist and the paramaguru (spiritual teacher's teacher) of Adi Shankaracharya.

Though the Mandukya is one of the shortest of major Upanishads, it has a distinct approach to the Vedantic teachings. It analyses the three states of humankind viz., waking (*jagrat*), dream (*svapna*) and dreamless sleep (*sushupti*) correlating these states to different types of human consciousness. Its conclusion appears in the maha vakya (great maxim), *ayamatma brahma* (this self is Brahman).

Gaudapada's Karika consists of four chapters. The first is concerned with the meaning of Om, which is an expatiation of the 12 passages of the Mandukya. The second chapter deals with proving the unreality of the phenomenal world. The third chapter establishes the truth of nonduality. This chapter is inserted lest the argument of negation in chapter 2 itself is not used against monism. The fourth chapter refutes all un-Vedic points of view which are inconsistent with non-dualism.

However, we shall only concentrate on the twelve passages constituting the Mandukya and their exposition by Gaudapada.

The very first stanza of the Upanishad asserts that the letter that is Om, is all this. All that is past, present or future is verily Om. And whatever is beyond the three periods of time is also Om. The author implies that Om is Brahman.

The second passage makes this explicit. All this is surely Brahman. This self is Brahman. The Self is possessed of four quarters. The Self is the one's innermost Self and is usually pointed out by placing one's hand on the heart.

The first quarter is Vaishvanara whose sphere of action is the waking state. Its consciousness relates to the things that are external; it has seven limbs and nineteen mouths and it enjoys gross things.

In the waking state one is absorbed in the external objects because of one's ignorance. It is believed that the heaven is the head, the sun is the eye, air is the vital force, space is the middle part, water is the bladder and the earth is the two feet of Vaishvanara self. His nineteen mouths are: five senses of perception, five organs of action, five pranas, mind, intellect, ego and mindstuff. Since these are the 'gates' of experience, they are called mouths. Vaishvanara is the *prathama* (first) quarter. It is called Vaishvanarah because he leads in diverse ways all (*vishva*) beings (*nara*) to their enjoyment. It is also called *sthulabhuk* or the enjoyer of the gross. It is also known as the first quarter or prathama pada and is the first step (pada) towards Brahman.

The fourth stanza mentions Taijasa as the second quarter whose sphere of action is the dream state. In this state the consciousness is internal and it enjoys the subtle objects. Though still in ignorance, Taijasa has lost contact with the external world and to it the cognition is in the form of a luminous (taijasa) thing. While Vishvanara depends on the external objects, Taijasa experiences 'impressions' and its enjoyment is subtle.

The fifth verse refers to the state of deep sleep. The sleeper does not enjoy things and sees no dreams. For him there is an undifferentiated mass of consciousness and abundant bliss. This state has been reached by passing through the waking and dreaming stages. This quarter is called Prajna.

The deep sleep is also called *anandamayah* or full of joy because there is no misery arising from the experience in which one is able to discern. There is extreme freedom. However, this is not the real Bliss which is yet to be attained.

The next verse says that Prajna is the Lord of all and is omniscient. It is the inner Director and the source of all. Prajna is the place of origin and dissolution of all beings.

Gaudapada comments that Vishva experiences and enjoys external gross things but is all-pervading. Taijasa experiences and enjoys internal things or the subtle. Prajna is a mass of consciousness and enjoys bliss (to be differentiated from the real Bliss). Enjoyment is thus three-fold corresponding to three states. According to him he, who has the knowledge of his three states and the kinds of joy he experiences is not affected in any way.

The Mandukya now moves on to the fourth quarter. The fourth quarter is that which is conscious neither of the inner world nor of the external world. It does not form a mass of consciousness. It is neither conscious nor unconscious. It is unseen, beyond empirical dealings, beyond the grasp of organs of senses or action. It can neither be inferred, nor described and is even unthinkable. Its only valid evidence is in the belief in the Self in which there are no phenomena. It is auspicious. That is the Self which is to be known.

The fourth state in which the phenomenal world disappears, is called Turiya. It may look strange that in Turiya, there is neither conciousness nor unconsciousness. Such contradictions often appear in Vedanta. With reference to the first three quarters we can speak of consciousness because they belong to the phenomenal world. Turiya is beyond this and its knowledge is Self. It is self-effulgent and does not require an external instrument of knowledge. It is the stage where duality vanishes.

Gaudapada's comments on this are interesting. The unchanging non-dual Lord Brahman is the ordainer in the matter of banishing sorrows. The effulgent, Turiya is the all-pervasive source of all objects.

Vishva and Taijasa are conditioned by cause and effect, Prajna is conditioned by cause. There is neither cause nor effect in Turiya. In Vishva and Taijasa there is misapprehension and non apprehension of Reality.

Prajna is caused by non apprehension of Reality. In Turiya neither misapprehension nor non apprehension can exist.

Gaudapada adds that Prajna does not comprehend anything—neither itself nor others, neither truth nor falsehood. Turiya according to him stands for everything. What's more, it is the witness.

Turiya is called *sarva-drik* or seer of everything for, ever. Turiya who exists in all beings during the dream and the waking states, is the seer. According to Brihadaranyaka Upanishad, "There is no witness but This."

Gaudapada makes a distinction between the non-perception of duality in case of Parjna and Turiya. Prajna is in sleep which is a causal state. In Turiya that sleep does not exist. Turiya being only a witness, there is no bondage in it. According to Gaudapada dream belongs to him whose perception is false, sleep belongs to the one who does not know Reality. Vishva and Taijasa are obstacles which need to be removed before one attains Turiya.

Man, awake, dreaming or under dreamless sleep is under the influence of the eternal maya. However, when he is awakened from the influence of maya, he realises the birthless, sleepless, dreamless non-dual Turiya or the Self.

Gaudapada has no doubt that the phenomenal world is the result of maya. Using contradictions, he says "All this is nothing but maya, is but non-duality in reality."

Mandukya asserts in the 8th verse that the Self when viewed from the standpoint of the syllable which denotes it, is Om. When you consider it from the standpoint of letters of which pranava is constituted

they are the quarters of the Self. There is no distinction
between the quarters and letters: a, u, m.

The Upanishad then compares Vaishvanara in the
waking state with the first letter 'a' because of being
pervasive ('a' is used most frequently) and the first.

He who is Taijasa (dream state) is the second letter
'u' because of excellence and the intermediate stage.

Prajna or the deep sleep is 'm'. Just as 'a' and 'u'
merge in 'm' when we pronounce AUM, Vishva and
Taijasa merge into Prajna.

According to Gaudapada, those who have understood
the similarities between the three states and three letters
are worthy of adoration.

'A' leads to Vishva, 'u' leads to Taijasa and 'm' leads
to Prajna. When Prajna disappears, the causal state is
destroyed; no attainment, no goal remains because you
have reached Turiya.

Mandukya's last verse is most illuminating. The
partless Om is Turiya which is beyond all conventional
dealings, the limit of the negation of the phenomenal
world. It is auspicious and non-dual. Surely it is Om,
the Self. He who understands this enters the Self through
his lower self.

The knower of the Self is the knower of Brahman.
He has reached Turiya by burning the first three states
and is not born again, because Turiya has no potential
for creation.

Gaudapada's concluding remarks on Om constitute
an excellent expatiation of Mandukya.

We should know Om, quarter by quarter because the
quarters of the Self are the letters of Om. When we have
known Om thus, we should not think of anything else.

You should concentrate your mind on Om. Om is
Brahman outside the region of fear. For a man who is

ever fixed in Brahman, there can be no fear anywhere. This is in consonance with the Vedic text.

"The enlightened man is not afraid of anything." (Taittiriya Upanishad 2 - 9).

In the 26th verse of Karika, Gaudapada asserts the equivalence in a strange way.

Om is surely the inferior Brahman and Om is considered to be the Superior Brahman. Om has no cause; it has no inside and outside and is without effect. It is undecaying. Gaudapada possibly refers to Om as the inferior Brahman because of the perception that Om is used merely as vehicle to attain Brahman. His reference to the Superior Brahman implies that Om is identical with Brahman.

Om is the beginning, middle and the end of everything. Having known Om, one immediately attains Self or Brahman.

One should know pranava to be God in the hearts of all. When the intelligent man meditates on the all-pervasive Om, he grieves no more. The reference to the heart is due to the belief that it is the seat of memory and perception.

Gaudapada concludes his disquisition on Om by asserting that Om is without measures. It is of infinite dimension. It is that auspicious entity where duality does not exist. One who knows Om is a sage. Without this knowledge no one can become a sage. When Gaudapada uses the term *amatrah* (beyond measures) in the context of Om, he is referring to Turiya.

Prashna

This short Upanishad belongs to the Atharvaveda. Shankara thinks it is a Brahmana complementary to Mantra Upanishad i.e., the Mundaka which, too, belongs to the same Veda. This Upanishad alone clearly mentions that creation originated from matter and energy.

Its name is derived from six *prashnas* or questions which were answered by rishi Pippalapada.

A group of students consisting of Sukeshas, Satyakama, Kausalya, Bhargava, and Kabandhin was in search of Brahman. It appears they were well established in the practice of devotion to the saguna Brahman or Hiranyagarbha. They, however, were interested in acquiring the knowledge of the Supreme Reality or nirguna Brahman. They went to the sage Pippalapada for guidance.

Pippalapada asked them to live again a year more in penance, abstinence and faith. He would answer their questions after the completion of this probationary period. It is presumed that the group obeyed the rishi and came back to him after one year. They asked him six questions to which the sage provided answers.

The first question relates to the creation of beings, the second pertains to the human personality, the third is concerned with the nature of prana, the fourth with human psychology, the fifth is about pranava or Om and the last relates to the metaphysical aspect of man. The questions are not all independent, but we shall discuss only the fifth prashna pertaining to pranava in detail.

Satyakama who is the son of Shibi asks the rishi :

"Respectable sir, which world is attained by a person who meditates upon Om until death?"

The rishi replies, "O Satyakama, Om is really the higher and the lower Brahman. Hence the person concerned attains either of the two. The higher Brahman refers to the unmanifest Absolute Reality. Hiranyagarbha is his first manifestation and thus is the lower Brahman. The sound Om emanates from Brahman. As we know it has 3½ moras (matras). The first three matras A-U-M, which are audible, represent the manifested state of Brahman while the half mora (ardha-matra) which is inaudible is the highest unmanifested Reality."

The rishi then adds that if the concerned person meditates upon one syllable, he returns to the world soon after his death, though he is enlightened. Riks transport him to the world of man, where he becomes great by living in austerity, continence and faith.

If a person meditates on two syllables, he is united with the mind after death i.e., he continues to live with his mental body or sukshmasharira. He is sent to the moon where he enjoys its splendour after which he returns to this world.

If a person meditates on the Supreme Purusha (Brahman) with Om consisting of three moras, he is united with the brilliant sun i.e., he attains *kramamukti.* He is freed from all sins in the same way as the snake who throws out its slough. He is transported to the world of Brahma by the Sama hymns. From this microcosmic self (Hiranyagarbha) he sees the Supreme Being residing in that heart.

When three matras are meditated upon separately, the meditator comes back to his world. However, when the matras are connected properly and meditated upon as a whole and are employed in a proper manner in the state of waking, sleeping, and dreaming, the practitioner becomes the 'knower' and he has no fear of anything.

By the Rik hymns (first matra) one attains this world, by the Yajus (second matra) one reaches the sky, the world of the moon. Through the Samans (third matra) one gains wisdom. Beyond the three matras is the fourth ardhamatra the inaudible sound which can be perceived only through great concentration. At this stage the person may be said to have imbibed the entire message of Om which is another way of saying that he attains the Supreme Brahman.

According to Swami Sarvananda, Om, the symbol of Brahman was the first sound produced at the beginning of the Creation. From the three matras of Om, emerged the 'feet' of Gayatri, and from these 'feet' appeared three Vedas and three worlds or vyahritis. From 'A' caused 'tat saviturvarenyam' which expanded itself to the Rigveda. From 'U' came 'bhargo devasya' which on expansion became the Yajurveda. From 'M' appeared 'dhiyo yo nah prachodayat' which expanded itself into the Samaveda. The first is hymnal (*stutipara*), the second is devoted to work (*kriyapara*) and the third is dedicated to knowledge (*jnanapara*).

Maitrayani

Maitrayani or Maitryopanishad is important because being one of the later Upanishads it quotes extensively from the earlier Upanishads.

In the second verse the Upanishad refers to Agni who is installed in the lotus of the heart and who is none other than the sun in the sky and is called *kala* (Time). The poet asks "Which is his lotus? What is his nature?" The poet himself provides the answer. "This sky is his lotus. The eight directions form its petals. They are close to Aditya (sun) and prana. These two should be worshipped with Om, vyahritis (bhuh, bhuvah, svah) and the Gayatri mantra." The verse shows a close connection between Om and the Gayatri.

In the 3rd stanza, the text maintains that Brahman has two forms, manifest and unmanifest. What is manifest is only an illusion. The unmanifest is the real Brahman. It is effulgence and is Aditya (sun) who has merged with Om with three matras a, u, m. The universe is woven with these matras. This Aditya must be meditated upon with Om and one should try to become one with him.

Note that this verse recognises only the unmanifest Brahman as Truth (satya). Nevertheless, the worshipper has to meditate upon its manifested forms, the sun and Om to realise the Ultimate Reality.

The next verse refers to the earlier Upanishads and Vedas and says that Udgitha is pranava and pranava is Udgitha. He is also Aditya. This pranava is named Udgitha, the engine of action, brilliant, sleepless, ever young—one which can be known in the state of waking, sleeping and deep sleep; prana, apana etc., and who is lodged in intelligence. This tripada Brahman has roots in the upper region; sky, Vayu, Agni, water and earth are its branches. Brahman is here compared with the Ashvattha tree which is inverted. The brilliance of Aditya and Om is a reflection of Brahman. Hence you should worship Brahman with Om which will help you realise Brahman. This syllable is the most sacred and he who knows it, can have any of his wishes fulfilled.

Verse 7 relates to the Gayatri. Initially this universe was soundless (*avyahrit*). Atman representing Truth and Prajapati, created through austerities (tapas) and meditation, the sounds bhuh, bhuvah and svah. This is a gross form of Prajapati whose body consists of svah (heaven, as the head), bhuvah (sky as the navel) and bhuh (earth as the feet). Aditya represents eyes which control man's destiny. These eyes are Truth. Those who meditate on these eyes are free to move in the real sense. Atman must, therefore, be worshipped with the vyahritis bhuh, bhuvah, svah. This has the effect of worshipping Prajapati, the Lord of the Universe and the Eyes of the Universe. It is believed that the body of Prajapati (mentioned above) holds the entire universe. Conversely, the entire universe contains Prajapati. Hence the worship of Atman is most fruitful.

The Upanishad again quotes earlier literature to elucidate the import of shabda Brahman and ashabda Brahman. Those who meditate have two optional Brahmans : the one with sound and the other soundless. The latter emanates from shabda Brahman which is nothing but Om. A person who repeats Om ascends and merges with the soundless or higher Brahman in the same way as the spider moves up while weaving his web. The person who meditates on Om attains liberation. Om in this verse appears like a ladder which can be used to reach the top, Brahman.

There are some scholars who describe the sound - Brahman in a different way. When you cover your ears with the palms, you hear a sound in the heart. This sound is associated with the sky and compared with the sounds of the flowing river, bell, utensil, wheel, croaking of the frog, rainfall and also the sound that appears at a quiet place. Those who meditate on Om cross all these Brahmic sounds and reach the unmanifest Brahman. They merge with Brahman in the same way as different fluids merge with honey and lose their identity. Both shabda Brahma and the higher *Parabrahma* are worth attaining. The person who becomes an adept in shabda Brahma can rise above and attain parabrahma.

In verse 23, the Upanishad again cites earlier literature and says that the shabda Brahman is Om. Its half-mora is Brahman. It is peace, bliss, satiated, stationary, stable, elixir like, immortal, formless and soundless. It is called Vishnu who is all-encompassing. For the highest place one should worship both Brahmans. The para as well as apara Brahman are Om. This soundless deity should be meditated at the head.

Verse 25 contends that those who withdraw their senses as one does when one is asleep or when one remains 'inside' the senses (as if in the dream-state) and sees Brahman called Om, who is the leader, effulgent, sleepless, who has no old age, who is immortal and who never despairs, acquires all these qualities himself.

One who conjoins prana, Om and all universes engages in the real yoga. Similarly when there is a merger of prana, mind and senses that state may be called yoga.

The Upanishad endorses an earlier work in which the body is equated with the bow and Om with its arrow, the mind with the tip of an arrow and tamas guna as the target. When this target is hit one can see what lies beyond - the brilliant Brahman which manifests itself in the shining sun. When you see this Brahman you become immortal.

Six

GANESHA

"Shri Ganeshaya namah"
"Sri Mahaganapataye namah"
("Obeisance to Ganesha"
"Obeisance to Great Ganapati")

Ganesha is usually invoked at the beginning of many mantras and rituals, and has precedence over other gods.

Ganesha is an elephant-headed god widely worshipped all over India. He is the son of Parvati and Shiva. According to a legend, when Parvati was having her bath, she asked her son to guard the entrance. Before Parvati completed her ablution, Shiva arrived at the scene and demanded that he should be admitted inside. Shiva does not seem to have recognised his own son. Ganesha, for whom his mother's instructions were precious, refused to admit Shiva. The angry father hurled his weapon *trishula* (trident) at his son, which decapitated the son. When Parvati finished the bath and came out, she was shocked to see her son beheaded by his father.

When the heart-broken Parvati told Shiva that Ganesha was her son who was guarding the place under her instructions, Shiva was crestfallen, but consoled his wife. He promised her to resurrect their son. The head of an elephant was brought and implanted on the torso of the dead son. Ganapati was brought to life again with an elephant's head. Ganesha, it must be mentioned, is invoked on all auspicious occasions and finds precedence over other gods when a number of deities are worshipped.

According to another legend, Ganesha was made from the scurf of Parvati's body. There is another story relating to Ganesha's elephant head. Parvati who was proud of her son asked Shani (Saturn), to look at the child. When Shani glanced at Ganapati, his head was burnt to ashes. Brahma asked Parvati to replace the head with the first she could find. The first head Parvati found, was an elephant's.

Ganapati is believed to have four or six arms, but there is no unanimity among scholars as to what he holds in his hands. According to one version, in one hand he holds a shell, in the second a discus, in the third a club or a goad and in the fourth a water lily.

Ganesha is called *Ekadanta* (*eka* for 'one' *danta* for 'tooth') because he has only one tusk. According to one legend, Parashurama, one of the incarnations of Vishnu, once came to Kailasa, the mountain which is Shiva's abode. He wanted to see Shiva who was at that time asleep. Ganesha obstructed Parashurama's entry into the inner quarters. Fighting broke out between the two gods. Ganesha appeared to have the advantage first, but Parashurama succeeded in throwing his axe at Ganesha. Ganesha recognised the axe as his father's weapon (which Shiva had gifted to Parashurama). In humility, Ganesha received the weapon on his tusk which was broken due to the impact.

Ganesha was not one of the earlier gods mentioned in chapter 2, when Aryans entered India. Today he is identified with Om or Brahman. The worship of the manifest form of the supreme God or Brahman is explained by Hindus as the first rung in the spiritual ladder. If idols of various gods are worshipped, it is because it is easy to meditate on the concrete rather than the abstract. Those who worship many gods treat this as a matter of practical means to reach Brahman rather than their belief in polytheism.

Ganesha and Om

Ganesha is so closely associated with Om that we may say that Om and Ganesha are the acoustic and visual aspects of the same Brahman.

Many people find a remarkable resemblance between the Sanskrit letter 'Om' and Ganesha. The left part of the letter is believed to resemble the head of Ganesha as well as A of AUM. The curl which appears on the right resembles the elephant's trunk.

According to Jnaneshvara, a 13th century saint who is famed for his commentary *Jnaneshvari* on the *Bhagavad Gita*, 'A' of AUM corresponds to the two legs in the typical posture Ganesha takes when he is squatting. The second letter U corresponds to the huge stomach which Ganesha is believed to possess. 'M' represents his crooked (*vakra*) mouth. He is also called *Vakratunda* (*tunda* for mouth).

It is believed that among all animals the elephant has the highest intelligence. Ganesha's elephant head is an indicator of his supreme intelligence and wisdom. The elephant's head is also believed to be a constant reminder to the worshipper, that though man has a high position in the animal kingdom, he should not forget that he retains his animal tendencies.

In Hindu pantheon most gods have a vehicle or *vahana* which is used by them for travelling. Ganesha's vahana is a mouse. The mouse represents undesirable tendencies in man and the huge god sitting on a small mouse indicates how Ganesha can subjugate wild passions. Many believers regard the rising sun as Om and the mouse as darkness. Ganesha's sitting on the mouse thus can be interpreted as dispelling darkness and ushering in the light.

According to tantra, the muladhara chakra is the abode of Ganesha. It is also believed to be the original place of Om. The muladhara contains the *bhumi* (earth) *tattva* (essence) and Ganapati is also supposed to be Mars, the son of the earth. The merger of bhumi tattva and *akasha* (sky) *tattva* represents liberation (moksha). Ganesha, the manifest Brahman, is believed to symbolise this moksha or possibly the way to attain moksha.

Ganapati is also identified with Brihaspati, the Lord of the Universe.

Ganapati's other name is supposed to be Brahmanaspati. Brahman, Udgitha, Om etc., all represent the same Ultimate Reality.

Hundreds of poems in honour of Ganapati have been composed. Recently a lawyer Deshpande composed a eulogy called 'shrimangalmurti stotra' in Sanskrit. The hymn is quite interesting and reflects the connection between Om and Ganesha.

The poet addresses Ganesha as *Gajanana*. ('gaja' for elephant, 'anana' for head). Gajanana is none other than another form of Om. He is not only truth but also Rita (the universal order). He is the 'adibija' or the first seed, i.e., Om. He is immortal. There is none greater than him.

In other words, he is Om or Brahman. He is not only the greatest among the great, he is also the minutest among the minute. This reflects advaitism or monism according to which Brahman is everywhere even in the minute part of space.

Gods and men both worship him and he is the God of learning. He desroys avidya (nescience) and extricates his worshippers from their predicaments. He has four hands. In one hand he holds a device with which he disentangles his worshippers from fetters. In another hand he holds a cookie called 'modaka' which is believed to be nourishing and makes one contented.[1] The third hand is used by Ganapati for blessing his worshippers. In his fourth hand Ganesha holds a goad with which he subdues the six enemies (*shadripu*) of his worshippers. The six traditional enemies of humankind are believed to be passion, anger, greed, conceit, envy and allurement. Freed from the inner enemies, his worshippers lead a selfless life which gives them true bliss.

Riddhi and Siddhi are Ganapati's wives. It is believed that they may arouse passion in the minds of the worshippers because of their association with their husband. Ganesha is believed to discipline his wives so that they do not create any allurement in the minds of his devotees who through their worship are trying to attain Om or Brahman.

Ganapati is believed to 'display' straight trunk to those who are guileless and a crooked trunk to those whose path is not in accordance with dharma. Ganesha has only one tusk. There are legends which suggest that the other tusk was broken in a fight. Those who have great faith in Gajanana, however, interpret one tusk as the symbol of the god's ability to stand alone (as one) and destroy maya which creates delusion.

He is called *Bhalachandra* ('bhala' for forehead and 'chandra' for moon) because on his forehead the moon showers his elixir-like rays.

As we have mentioned earlier, the mouse is his vahana. This mouse is sometimes compared with Time (*kala*) who, like a rat, destroys everything clandestinely. Ganapati controls Time by making it his vehicle.

Ganesha, as we have said, rests basically at the muladhara. Yogis worship him with Om, which illuminates the manipura and other chakras (see the chapter on tantra) and the yogi attains supreme bliss and realises Brahman.

There are many yantras associated with Ganesha. In each of the yantras Om is either inscribed or hinted at.

There are hundreds of mantras associated with Ganapati. Some of these mantras are used for specific purposes. Om appears several times in most of these mantras. One also finds Ganesha referred to by different names. Only a brief sketch of these mantras is given below.

1. *Shriganapati mantra* in which Om appears almost in every line. It also gives a japa mantra in which Ganesha is referred to as Gajakarna (having the ears like those of elephant), Lambodara (one with huge stomach), Vighnanashi (one who destroys obstacles), Bhalachandra (having the moon on the forehead.)

2. *Shripranavarupa Ganesha.* The title itself suggests that Ganesha is Om (pranava) or Brahman. This mantra is believed to bestow immortality, wealth and knowledge on the worshipper.

3. *Uchhishta Ganapati -mantra.* In this the god is referred to as Ganesh Rishi, Ekadanta, Hastimukha (having the face of the elephant). Besides Om, other bijas like gam, hum, klaum, etc., also appear.

4. *Shakti-Vinayaka Ganapati Mantra.* In this, Ganapati is sought for shakti or power.Vinayaka is his another name. Besides Om being prefixed to every line, a number of bijas follow Om such as gram, grim, grum etc.

5. *Kamana - Siddhaye Kechana Ganesha Mantra.* This should be obtained only from a Guru, and is to be used for the fulfilment of a wish. There are a number of variants of this mantra according to the concerned purpose :

   (a) For acquiring knowledge
   (b) For getting a husband
   (c) For trouble-shooting
   (d) For controlling pests, rats, etc.
   (e) For rains
   (f) For seduction
   (g) For destruction of the evil
   (h) For good health
   (i) For averting any danger
   (j) For recovering lost wealth
   (k) For recovering lost animals
   (l) For acquiring brilliance
   (m) For acquiring agricultural land.
   (n) For begetting a son.

The mechanics of the mantras to be used for the worship of Ganesha is too complex to be detailed here. Four characteristics, however, may be mentioned.

1. Om is the most prominent bija mantra which is sometimes coupled with other bijas.

2. Ganapati is mentioned by different appellations.
3. Mantras are repeated several times, sometimes as many as 10,000 times.
4. The influence of tantra is manifest from certain bijas which are found in tantric worship. Nevertheless, Om is the 'adibija' or the first seed.

Before we conclude the synopsis of Ganesha mantras we should mention the Chintamani Mantra. Chintamani is another name of Ganesha. In the mantra, both Ganesha's father Shiva and mother Uma are invoked.

According to a legend, Indra was cursed by Gautama Rishi and had 1000 dents or distortions on his body. Indra worshiped Ganesha who converted the dents into 1000 eyes.

In India there are 21 idols of Ganesha (including Chintamani) which are self-generated (*svayambhu*).

With his trunk and large ears Ganesha would appear to the scholars of religion as the appropriate god of phallus worship. In humour, the baby boy is often referred to as Ganapati or the elephant's trunk. However, surprisingly Ganapati is not worshipped specially in connection with phallus or fertility. It is Ganesha's father Shiva who is worshipped symbolically as linga (phallus). The symbol appears as a column of stone, a cone of mud and even the icy formation of a similar symbol in the cold Himalayas. We do not know if there is any connection between the phallic worship of Shiva and the suggestive head of Ganapati, which according to the legend was implanted by Shiva.

Ganesha in Tantra

Ganesha has great importance in tantra. *Gana* means individual beings, discrete divine bodies, unique forces or sometimes lesser gods. *Isha* means one who can do what he wants, and undo what others have done. Ganas also mean demigods attending Shiva. Ganesha is interpreted as the Almighty Lord, who lives eternally in the Mother's womb.

According to the kundalini yoga, muladhara (see the chapter on tantra) is his place of abode. From there he controls all chakras and the wheel of life. His large head symbolises knowledge and he is called *Brahmanaspati* or the Lord of knowledge and intelligence. His large belly is believed to indicate his capacity to devour the whole universe that evolves from the Divine Mother.

He is believed to control the karmic law for which he is called Kama Adhyaksha ('Adhyaksha' for president). His big ears symbolise his capacity to hear every sound; no prayer can escape his attention.

Ganesha's head is believed to contain 'sweet' intelligence. The fluid which flows through the temporal gland of male elephants, is ever present in Ganapati as a result of which bees are believed to be attracted to the sweet aroma emanating from him.

His eyes are small because he does not require them, he (like his father Shiva) has a third eye through which he can see the past, the present and the future. He is, therefore, called *Adi Rishi* ('Adi' for first 'Rishi' for seer).

In tantra he is associated with Om for many reasons. Om being the source of all mantras, chanting Om is equivalent to meditating on Ganesha. Further, the muladhara is also supposed to be the place where sounds, mantras and words lie in the dormant stage. Ganesha's role in tantra will be discussd in the chapter on tantra.

It would be instructive to mention *Ganesha Gita*. This is a text used by Ganapatayas or the worshippers of Ganapati. It is nothing but the *Bhagvad Gita* in which the name Ganesha is substituted for that of Krishna who is an incarnation of Vishnu, but who is identified with Brahman in the *Bhagvad Gita*. This is quite consistent with the conception that Atman, Brahman, Ganesha and Om are identical with the Ultimate Reality.

There are many yantras (geometrical figures) used in the worship of Ganesha. The following figure shows a yantra for worship (*upasana*).

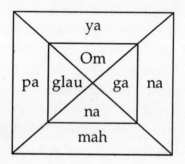

Worship Ritual

We will be able to gauge the importance of Ganesha, if we consider worship ritual which is called *pujanam* or *puja*. A puja can be very short and simple or very long and complex involving many rituals.

A major puja is usually conducted to worship a god who is the main deity of the puja. While the puja consists of several rituals, one of the rituals is usually the puja of Ganesha. It is difficult to think of a major puja which does not contain the Ganesha puja as a constituent element. This puja of Ganapati is thus a puja within the main puja. This leads to an interesting case in which Ganesha himself is the main deity. For example, in Ganesha Chaturthi, which is a worship ceremony celebrated on the birthday of Ganapati, there are two pujas related to Ganapati; one is the usual mandatory Ganesha puja which appears in the pujas of all gods, and the other is the puja of the main deity which in this case happens to be Ganesha Himself.

The traditional scriptures prescribe over forty samskaras, many of which are rites of passage such as initiation, marriage and funeral rites. Ganapati pujanam appears as one of the subsidiary rituals in most of these samskaras, though its structure may slightly vary depending on the nature of the main ceremony.

Seven

OM SHANTIH SHANTIH SHANTIH !

"There are two methods of pacifying the mind, Yoga and Jnana (knowledge)."

—Yoga Vasishtha (5-78-8)

Sarasvati is the goddess of knowledge. She is usually associated with a stringed instrument called veena. Those who play this veena or a similar instrument usually adjust the keys to Om and are believed to 'see' the syllable.

Ancient rishis called Sarasvati's veena shanti which means peace. Om resembles 'hum', a syllable uttered to indicate one's consent (equivalent to yes or ok) Vinoba Bhave interprets this as indicating peace. According to him there is an intimate relationship between Om and peace. This is the reason why singers and instrumentalists chant 'Om shantih shantih shantih' before they begin their practice.

We have seen that there are various meanings of A-U-M. The last half matra indicates the turiya state which is equivalent to samadhi and absolute silence. The ancient sages emphasised that peace is absolutely necessary to attain this last state which is nothing but Brahman.

According to the Chhandogya Upanishad (3-14-1), since everything is 'tajjalan' it is Brahman and hence it behoves you to worship and meditate in peace. Bhave translates 'tajjalan' as 'one which is born of, controlled by and merges with Brahman'. According to Bhave peace cannot be divorced from Brahman.

We have seen that Om is called 'Udgitha' which seems to mean 'supreme song' or 'supreme praise'. According to Bhave its etymology can be traced to the roots ut(generation), gih (merger), and tham (state), and corresponds to the three matras of Om. Udgitha, shanti, Brahman and Om all indicate the Ultimate Reality.

According to a legend there was a war between gods (devas) and demons (*asuras*). Gods surrendered to Udgitha and worshipped it thinking that it was prana flowing through the nose. Asuras hurled 'sins' against the nose with the result that prana was cursed and even the sweet odor turned into a stench. Devas then worshipped speech identifying it with Udgitha. Asuras repeated their experiment with the tongue with the result that speech become defective. Gods then tried eyes, ears and mind which were equally subjugated by asuras. When gods realised that Udgitha is the principal prana or Brahman, they worshipped the Ultimate Truth. Asuras' weapons were ineffective. Udgitha came to be known as a deity called *dur* which signified that death could not come near Udgitha.

Those who feel, they have committed a sin, are advised to worship Udgitha, Om, shanti (peace) which are different names of the same Brahman. Earlier shanti was called 'sham' and hence Om was called Shankara or Shambhu, which are the names of Shiva. In Kenopanishad, Om is called Uma (Shiva's wife). Thus Uma and Shankara may be said to be two aspects of Om.

Rishabha, Ganesha, Soma (moon) Uma, Shiva all seem to represent Om as well as shanti.

The principal prana is the life-force and is not different from Om or Udgitha. At the universal level the life-force appears as shanti which is non-dual or the Ultimate Truth. Goddess Aditi is the combination of shaktis (powers) and appears when Om or Atman is worshipped. She enters the heart (cave) and appears in different forms to different living beings. Aditi is the uniting force and epitomises non-dualism.

Many people mistake shanti or nivritti or mukti (liberation) for inaction. There is a difference between, say, a stone and a yogi. Both display peace and inactivity. The former, however, is dead in the real sense while the latter is striving to attain liberation. Similarly a karmayogi or the person who works without attachment or without expecting any fruits of his action may appear hyperactive - but shanti reigns in him - it is the kind of peace which leads him to Brahman.

Peace is not only a tool of the worship of Om, it is also its nature and goal. One càn therefore regard shanti and Om as synonymous. A sage was asked 'What is the nature of Atman?' to which he merely nodded. Since the questioner did not understand his non-verbal communication, the sage added, "Peace inheres in Atman".

According to Bhave, the import of the verse in the *Bhagvad Gita*, "Atman does not kill, he is not killed, nor does he effect killing through an agency" represents three aspects of peace. According to a legend, gods, men and demons went to Prajapati. Prajapati uttered 'da' to every group. Gods rightly interpreted it as the subjugation of passion (*damana*), men interpreted it as

charity (*dana*) and demons construed it as mercy (*daya*).
In fact Prajapati was telling all groups to curb their evil
tendencies hinting at their respective weakness.
According to Bhave the three letters A-U-M stand
for damana, dana, and daya. Beyond these three lies
the half matra which is *shantatman*, where peace and
Atman coalesce.

The utterance of shantih three times has been
interpreted in several ways. Rishi Vasishtha considers
the triple shanti equivalent to the three eyes of
Tryambaka (Shiva). In the Rigveda one finds a verse to
the effect that we worship the three-eyed Shiva who has
conquered passion, anger and greed. We worship his
peaceful (soothing) brilliance. We hope that we will be
free from death and continue to drink the elixir of peace.

The ancient rishis regarded peace and Om
inseparable. It is believed that in the heart of Shiva lies
Vishnu and in the heart of Vishnu is Shiva. The sages
thought that a similar paradox prevailed in case of
shanti and Om. The former was inside the latter and
the latter inside the former.

Chapter 36 of the Yajurveda is called 'Shantirpathartha'.
The first mantra appears as below:

I surrender to the Rigveda which is speech, Yajur
which is mind and Sam which is prana and eyes,
(*chakshu shrotra*)

There is no direct reference to Om in the verse, but
Bhave interprets speech as A, mind as U and prana as
M of AUM.

The second mantra is as follows:

We pray that any deficiency in our eyes, heart and
mind may be rectified by Brahaspati's blessings.
O Brahaspati, the Master of all, bless us.

This is interpreted by Bhave as a prayer to Brahaspati for peace (shanti) According to him the search for shanti is tantamount to seeking Om because Brahaspati is none other than Brahmanaspati or Ganapati(Ganesha) who is identified with Om. The 17th mantra reads as:

"Let the heaven, sky and earth give us peace. Let waters, medicinal herbs and other flora, Vishva Deva, Brahman and the universe be filled with shanti! That which is veritably shanti will give peace to us."

While peace is explicitly mentioned here, Om is interpreted through bhuh (earth), bhuvah (sky) and suvah (heaven) which stand for A, U, M respectively.

The three mantras when read together are interpreted to mean that peace and Om are inseparable.

In 17th mantra appear the words 'shantireva shantih' which Bhave treats as the definition of shanti by ancient rishis. The words mean 'shanti itself is shanti' or 'shanti is shanti'. This definition appears circular but according to Bhave it indicates the uniqueness of shanti.

Shanti implies fearlessness and is the very antithesis of chaos or lawlessness. Bhave has liberally interpreted a verse from the Atharvaveda (19-15-56):

"We pray that the earth, sky and heaven (which represent the three matras A-U-M and are synonymous with shanti) will make us fearless. In our spiritual journey we may go ahead smoothly or lag behind, we may climb up and then fall, but the setbacks will not daunt us. We hope to get moral support from our known friends as well as unknown people. The knowledge of our past mistakes and the lack of knowledge of the future mistakes will not frighten us. Our collective determination will be our strength."

As we mentioned earlier, peace implies consent and non-resistance. Rishi Yajnavalkya once said that under the rule of Om, various rivers emanating from the Himalayas flow in different directions according to their wish; some go to the east, some flow to the west. The phenomenon displays peaceful consent and complete rapport with Om. The sage adds that this Om or *akshara* (immortal) never destroys nor is destroyed. It is thus a two-fold shanti.

A verse which appears in the Yajurveda twice is believed to display a connection between the worship of Om, karma yoga and shanti.

"Since we want to progress with sadhana, we pray to the cosmic karma yogi Vachaspati (Brahaspati). Since his very existence is meant to protect others, it is his duty to respond to our supplication. He is the ocean of peace (shambhu or Shiva) and is the repository of good deeds."

Sham-bhu is believed to indicate Om which is nothing but the ocean of peace.

Om Tat Sat

Om tat sat is a well-known expression. Om stands for Brahman or what is approved by Ishvara (God), *sat* stands for truth or good deeds dictated by dharma. *Tat* represents karma yoga or action without any expectation of fruits.

We mentioned earlier that there are three gunas viz., sattva, rajas and tamas. It is not permissible to interpret *tat* as action which is rajas or tamas merely because it shows lack of interest. Om and sat make it mandatory that the action which constitutes karma yoga should not be sinful. What this implies is that a misdeed cannot be condoned under the excuse that it is done in a disinterested manner.

The closing verses of the Yajurveda are interesting:

The vital prana (Vayu) constitutes the immortal part of man, the body turns to ashes. 'O! Om (Brahman), I wish to obtain the highest world by remembering my past deeds.' (40-17)

O Agni, you know our deeds. Liberate those of us who have done disinterested deeds. Keep sins away from us. Obeisance to you (forgive us), we cannot perform such acts as yajna when our body is no more. (40-18)

Brilliance engulfs the true Brahman. I am the Purusha (man) who appears as Aditya. This pranava (Om) like the sky is all-encompassing and Brahman.

In all these mantras Om appears explicitly. Moreover the three matras of pranava AUM are identified with Vayu (40-17), Agni (40-18), sun or Aditya (40-19)

The Yajurveda ends with the words 'Om kham Brahma'. The word 'kham' is connected with a legend. One Upakosala worshipped three Agnis for 12 years. The Agnis are believed to have given a mantra to the brahmacharin "Prano Brahma, kam Brahma, kham Brahma' or 'Atman is Brahman, kam is Brahman, kham is Brahman." When the worshipper pleaded his ignorance about the meaning of kam Brahma, kham Brahma." The Agnis replied, "Kam is kham and kham is kam." Om, Brahma (Brahman), kam, kham all seem to be synonymous. Kham is usually used to designate the sky.

Bhave wonders why the closing verse uses 'Om kham Brahma' rather than 'Om kam Brahma'. His interpretion is that kham is closer to the sky than kam. The sky is inert in the sense it offers no resistance and thus epitomises peace or shanti. By placing kham between Om and Brahman, the Veda is merely identifying shanti with both Om and Brahman.

Ka has been interpreted as happiness in Upanishads. In the Chhandogya Upanishad ka and kha appear to be united. "If there were no *sky* which is *happiness* how would breathing (prana) be possible?"

Bhave concludes that the message which the Agni delivered to Upakosala consisted of three truths.

1   Atman or prana is necessary for the worship of Om.
2. Shanti or kham signifies the sadhana of Om.
3. Happiness—kam is the fruit of the worship of Om.

Eight

BHAGAVAD GITA

"To one who has studied the *Bhagavad Gita* even a little, who has sipped at least a drop of the Ganges water, who has worshipped at least once Lord Murari (Destroyer of ego) to him there is no disputation (quarrel) with Yama, the God of Death. Seek Govindam...."

- Shankara's *Bhaja Govindam* (20)

The *Mahabharata* is one of the sacred books of Hindus and the longest epic in the world containing 110,000 couplets. Composed in the first millenium BCE, it depicts a great war between the Kurus and Pandus—two branches of the same family. However, it is treated as an allegory dentifying the former with the spirits of evil and the latter with the spirits of good.

The *Bhagavad Gita* ('The song of the lord') is a poem which is part of the *Mahabharata*. It is a dialogue between prince Arjuna of Pandavas and Lord Krishna who is also his charioteer. Ostensibly, it is Krishna's exhortation to Arjuna who has a moral dilemma when he is required to kill his own cousins, to do his duty rising above the sentimental bonds. However, the *Bhagavad Gita* which contains eighteen chapters, imparts knowledge of eighteen yogas which can help one attain liberation. Highly venerated by Hindus, it is sometimes treated as the fifth Veda. Many scholars believe that the eighteen yogas can be reduced to four viz., karma yoga, raja yoga, jnana yoga and bhakti yoga.

In most of the chapters, Om is compared with either Brahman, the Ultimate Reality or its precious creations which are sometimes equated with Brahman.

In *jnana vijnana yoga* (the yoga of knowledge and realisation), Krishna asks Arjuna to take refuge in him saying:

"O son of Kunti, I am the sapidity (rasa) in water, the radiance in the moon and the sun. I am the syllable Om (pranava) in all the Vedas, sound in ether and manliness in man."

(VII 8)

In the whole chapter Krishna describes how he manifests in different forms. Evidently he is to be taken as Brahman. Om is thus the Brahman in all Vedas. Ether is believed to be the vehicle of sound which is modified into different languages. Om is the synthesis of all the manifestations of sound.

In *akshara brahma yoga* or the yoga of imperishable Brahman, Krishna mentions how a dying man can attain moksha.

All the gates of the body closed, the mind concentrated in the heart, fixing life-energy in the head, established in yoga, chanting the monosyllable Om (Brahman), thinking of me, he who leaves his body attains the Supreme goal. (8-12-13)

In this stanza the identification of Om with Brahman is explicit. Needless to say, Krishna identifies himself with Brahman. While departing from the body, utterance of Om is believed to create vibrations which make the dying man experience infinite bliss and the radiance of the pure consciousness. The Supreme goal which the yogi attains is called *Brahmanirvanam*. This is also called *aparoksha anubhuti*. The yogi merges with Brahman.

In *rajavidya rajaguhya yoga* or the yoga of sovereign science and sovereign secret, Krishna says:

> I am the Father and Mother of the world, the dispenser and the grandfather. I am the knowable and the purifier. I am the syllable Om and also Rik, Saman and Yajus. (9-17)

It is interesting to see that the fourth Veda, Atharva is not mentioned. This can be interpreted in two ways :

(1) The Atharva does not have the exalted status of the first three Vedas.

or

(2) The Atharva was composed subsequent to the *Mahabharata*.

Languages are believed to be based on the science of sound which expresses itself with perfection in the Vedas. Sound is also called God or *Nadabrahman*. As we pointed out earlier, sound is eternal, symbolised by Om, which can be analysed as A-U-M—A epitomises the origin, U the sustenances and M the termination.

In *Vibhuti yoga* or the yoga of divine manifestation, Krishna mentions several manifestations of Brahman :

"Among the great rishis I am Bhrigu. Of utterances I am the monosyllable Om. Of yajnas I am japayajna. Among the stationary things I am the Himalaya."

The triad Om-Krishna-Brahman appears again in this stanza. It is also important to remember that rishis or seers, yajna and japa are closely connected with Om. It would be unthinkable to divorce them from pranava.

In the same yoga, Krishna adds:

> Among letters I am 'A', among the compound words I am dvandva (dual) I am everlasting Time. I am the Dispenser facing on all sides. (X, 33)

The Ultimate Reality is unmanifest. When manifest, Brahman appears as Nada Brahman (*nada* for sound). The entire universe is formed out of this primordial sound. In Sanskrit the word *pada-artha* implies a word with its meaning. The whole acoustic reality is nothing but Om. As mentioned earlier the first part of this pranava is 'A' (A-U-M). It is also the first letter in most alphabets and is equated with Brahman.

Om Tat Sat

In *shraddhatraya vibhaga yoga*, or the yoga of three-fold faith, Arjuna asks Krishna how the evil attached to even the holiest deeds (karmas) such as yajna, gift(dana), and austerity (tapas) can be wiped out. Krishna's reply is:

> "Om Tat Sat. This has been proclaimed as the three-fold appellation of Brahman. By that were made the Brahmanas, Vedas and Yajnas. Hence the acts of sacrifice, gift and austerity should be made with the utterance of Om as provided in the scriptures, by those who follow the Vedas."   (XVII, 23, 24)

Om Tat Sat is a triplet which appears frequently in scriptures. All those three words mean Brahman. As mentioned earlier, Brahman manifests itself as sound and then as the universe. The totality of the sound is Om which is Nada Brahman. *Tat* means 'It' and refers to Brahman. 'It' is not used to refer to a man or woman. *Sat* means the Ultimate Reality which is not bound by space, time or causation.

Though everything is Brahman, there are a few things which indicate the stamp of their Creator; those precious creatures like brahmins who are believed to be most evolved spiritually among men, the Vedas which are the most superior among different branches of knowledge, and yajnas the most precious activity man can perform.

Om, the Nada Brahman emanating from the unmanifest Brahman, brahmins, the Vedas and yajnas have a place of honour.

It is believed that no karma is perfect. But we cannot renounce actions, which the duty binds us to perform. In order to eradicate the evil from the imperfect deeds, 'Om' should be uttered before we do our karmic duty.

The utterance of Om introduces an element of divinity and makes our actions in harmony with nature. Our actions translate themselves into a divine purpose and thus help us ascend to a higher level.

This principle of using the device for wiping out the evil seems to have led to the worship of Ganesha who is known as Vighnaharta or the remover of obstacles. Ganesha is invoked on all auspicious occasions and his worship precedes the worship of the main deity in a puja. Ganesha thus may be called an idol surrogate of the primordial sound Om.

We may summarise the status of Om in the *Bhagavad Gita* as follows:

1. At the lowest level, Om is used to purify our actions or make them perfect. It is also used as a means to reach Brahman by the dying man who utters Om continuously thinking of Krishna.

2. At the next level it is treated as the sum total of the sound created by the Unmanifest when it becomes manifest or Nadabrahman and creates the entire universe.

3. At the highest level Om is nothing but Brahman whose manifestation is Krishna.

It is intriguing that Om is not prescribed or emphasised in other yogas of the *Bhagavad Gita*. For example, in dhyana yoga or the yoga of meditation, Krishna asks the yogi to meditate on him (Krishna). But since Krishna identifies himself with the Supreme Being, its equivalent Om, does not seem to be necessary.

Jnaneshvara (Dnyaneshvar)

Jnaneshvara was a saint born in the state of Maharashtra in the 13th century. He wrote a commentary on the *Bhagavad Gita* at the age of 15 or 16. He is believed to have performed many miracles. Though we may treat the anecdotes of his supernatural powers as apocryphal, there is no doubt that he was a genius. His work *Jnaneshvari* which is a commentary on the *Bhagavad Gita* is a masterpiece, a testimony of his intellectual prowess.

In the first chapter, Jnaneshvara salutes Ganesha whom he identifies with Om, and Sarasvati.

Om is the beginning of this world. The Vedas describe it at length and it is Paramatman (Brahman). It is that which can analyse itself. I salute this Om. Oh revered Ganesha, Om is your manifestation. You enlighten us.

Jnaneshvera is a poet par excellence and uses a metaphorical language. The form of Ganesha is *shabdabrahma* (*shabda* for sound, *Brahma* for God) or the Vedas. The matras or letters are his beautiful and pure body. Manusmriti, Parasharasmriti, Yajnavalkyasmriti etc., are the different parts of his body. (A smriti is 'what was remembered', for instance, such works as Puranas, Sutras, Vedangas and writings by sages).

The meaning of the smritis is Ganeshas' glory. The eighteen Puranas are his jewelry. In chhandas (meters) we find the gems of philosophy. Poetry and drama are the small bells Ganesha wears around his feet. From these bells flows the music which is full of meaning.

Ganapati's six arms are the six darshanas viz., Samkhya, Yoga, Nyaya, Vaisheshika, Mimamsa and Vedanta. These philosophies are the weapons in his hands. Anumana (inference) is the axe, the sixteen padarthabhedas (categories) are his goad, the essence of the Vedanta is the modaka (a sweet cookie which he likes). The defeated Buddhism is symbolised by his broken tusk. He holds this broken tooth in his hand as Yoga. He is blessed by Sankhya and protected by Jaimini's *Dharmasutras*.

His trunk symbolises the Supreme Bliss (*brahmananda*) and also the power of discrimination. His tiny eyes indicate his wisdom and his ears symbolise Purva Mimamsa and Uttara Mimamsa (Vedanta). Both dualism and non-dualism of the Vedanta are on his head. Ten Upanishads are the flowers on his crown.

Omkara is Ganesha. Om or AUM consists of 3 1/2 moras A (his feet), U (his belly, *udara*), M (his head, or *mastaka*) With the half matra, Om is the primordial sound or Brahman. Om is the Vedas and the most sacred manifest form of Ganesha.

In chapter 6 on dhyana yoga of the *Bhagavad Gita*, Krishna explains to Arjuna that a yogi has to strive assiduously and purify himself from sins and has to pass through many births to reach perfection. He can then attain the Supreme Goal.   (B G 6-45)

Jnaneshvara comments on this as follows :

When such a person undergoes several births, the doors of moksha (liberation) are open to him. The mind is like a cloud and thinking like a wind, but for such a yogi both obstacles disappear. What remains is the sky of Brahman. The yogi reaches the turiya state of the half matra of Om. At this place no sound can reach. Brahman, though the mover of all movements, is ever stable. The yogi thus becomes immovable and eternal Brahman.

In chapter 7 (jnana vijnana yoga) Krishna refers to himself as the eternal seed :

O Partha, know me as the eternal seed of all beings; I am the intelligence of the intelligent; the glory of the glorious.   (B G 7-10)

Jnaneshvara comments that this seed is the adibija (primal seed). At the beginning this adibija sprouted first into akasha (sky) - This adibija devours even the Omkara (the primordial sound) and appears as the manifest world and is also the unmanifest Brahman.

Expatiating on Krishna's discourse to Arjuna in chapter 10 (Vibhuti yoga), Jnaneshvara says:

The wise worshippers know that they are born because of Krishna. They are contented because he is their life force. These bhaktas chant Krishna's japa loudly. In fact, they proclaim to the world aloud what a guru transmits to his disciple secretly, viz., the mantra of Om. Just as the poor or the rich can smell the sweet odour of a flower they spread the message of pranava to all irrespective of their station in life.

In chapter 11 (vishvarupa darshana yoga), Krishna endows Arjuna with the power to see the former's Great Form which is awesome. Jnaneshvara's interpretation of some of the stanzas is quite interesting. Krishna is Brahman. He is beyond the 3 1/2 matras of Om or pranava.

Shraddhas

In Chapter 17, Krishna elaborates three types of *shraddhas* (faith)—*sattvika, rajasika* and *tamasika*. The sattvika group worships Paramatman who manifests as Shiva, Vishnu, Ambika, Ganesha etc. The rajasika type venerates the deities having the properties of the manifestations, failing to recognise that they are all Brahman. The tamasikas are lazy and ignorant and worship deities who enjoy injuring others.

Krishna also mentions sattvika, rajasika and tamasika yajnas, austerities and gifts.

Jnaneshvara explains Krishna's advice to Arjuna succinctly :

You should discard the rajasika and tamasika aspect and embrace what is sattvika. The sattvika deeds will yield excellent fruits. But this is not the final goal. The essence of liberation (moksha) is different. It is only when the sattvika deeds are associated with Om Tat Sat - the sign of Brahman that the sattvika karma leads you to Brahman.

Brahman really does not have any appellation, but for common people the Vedas have given three names to it; Om, Tat and Sat. There is no communication channel between ordinary beings and God. To fill this lacuna, Father Veda has created these syllables. If you utter any one of these syllables, you should expect cognisance of your prayer from Brahman.

Those who live in the city of Upanishads situated on the mountains of the Vedas are sages who know the greatness of these three syllables. It is these syllables which prompted Brahma to create the world. Om is the first, Tat is the second and Sat is the third name. If you do your duty in association with these symbols you can attain liberation (moksha). However, you must know how these symbols should be properly used.

Arjuna, one should utter Om before one starts work. First, you must meditate on Om, then yajna, tapas or dana must be undertaken with sattvika attitude. This helps you like a light that does not extinguish in darkness or a strong friend who accompanies you on an unknown path. By the deeds like yajna, no doubt you will earn merit . But to enjoy its fruits you have to pass through the heaven and rebirth. These stages can be eliminated if you utter Om at the very beginning of a task. Pranava is like a boat which can help you cross a stream.

The wise people do not accept the fruits of yajna, they offer it to Brahma that is Tat. You should use 'Tat' for renunciation of the fruits of action.

With Om at the beginning and Tat after the deed, your work becomes deified but dualism does not disappear. When you add salt to water, the salt is not destroyed, it appears in the changed taste of water. Similarly with only Om and Tat the gulf between you and Brahman is not bridged; the duality still exists.

In order to identify yourselves with Brahman you should use the third syllable Sat. With this word you see and become Brahman.

When you perform good deeds you may violate the prescribed rules inadvertently. In our daily life it is not always possible to do our duty with perfection. 'Sat' is the word which exhonerates you from any deviations and helps you attain Brahman.

Arjuna, this three-fold appellation is Brahman. 'Om Tat Sat' is Brahman which is beyond gunas (qualities) and forms. Just as the sun cannot exist without its rays —without this triplet in dana, yajna or tapas Brahman cannot be conceived of. O Arjuna, if you discard 'Om Tat Sat' and perform great deeds like Ashvamedha yajna or do tapas by standing on one toe, or construct many water tanks for people, donate invaluable gems, all these deeds will go waste. Remember, you cannot embrace your own shadow, slap the sky or allow huge stones to pass through a sieve. Never do any deed without shraddha. What Krishna implies is that broadly there are two types of goals, impossible and possible. In the first type are the unattainable goals such as embracing one's shadow. The other type viz., attainable goals can be touched only when you want to attain Brahman, the use of Om Tat Sat as mentioned above constitutes an essential component of shraddha or faith.

Nine

OM AND THE GAYATRI

"The wise and the bold use the sacrificial objects and hymns
for worshipping Savita."

—(Rigveda 3-62-12)

While Om is Brahman, the Ultimate Reality, it is inextricably linked with peace (shanti), the Gayatri mantra and some other words whose identity sometimes appears to merge with Om.

The Gayatri is one of the most sacred mantras, which is taught to the initiate at the time of the thread ceremony (upanayana). The mantra worships Savita or Suryanarayana (the sun) and is associated with rishi Vishvamitra. Gayatri is actually the meter of the mantra.

The mantra appears in the Rig, Yajus and Sama. The original mantra appears in the Rig as follows :

Tat Saviturvarenyam bhargo devasya dhimahi
Dhiyo yo nah prachodayat.

(RV 3-62-10)

Three additional words are prefixed to the above in the Yajurveda:
Bhuh bhuvah svah,
The mantra means:

We contemplate the adorable glory of the deity which inheres in the earth, sky and heaven. May that stimulate our mental powers.

The deity Savita epitomises the power of light.

Bhuh bhuvah svah (earth, sky, heaven) which do not appear in the original mantra are called the vyahritis which are also identified with a, u, m of Aum. They are also considered as prana, apana and vyana, the components of the main prana (also called prana) or life-force. Agni, Vayu and Surya are believed to be the deities of the earth, sky and heaven.

A commentary, *Vedangaghantu*, elaborates the meaning of the vyahritis and mentions 52, 68 and 31 devatas associated with them. A person who chants the vyahritis, in fact, invokes 151 deities.

It is also believed that the 24 letters of the Gayatri are associated with specific parts of the body and specific devatas. Each letter is believed to endow the worshipper with a specific power.

The Methods of the Gayatri Japa

As we mentioned earlier Om is invariably associated with the Gayatri. The association, however, stems from many combinations which give us a number of different Gayatris.

The mantra is chanted loudly (*upanshu*) or chanted mentally (*manasikah*)

1. When only one Om is prefixed, the japa is called *ekapada*. This would appear as.
   Om bhurbhuvah ... prachadoyat.
   It is believed that this japa can cure such diseases as diabetes.
2. When Om is prefixed and suffixed to the complete Gayatri, the japa appears as Om... prachodayat Om which is called *samputa japa*, and is believed to cure mental diseases.

3. The *tripada japa* in which Om appears thrice is
   Om bhurbhuvah svah Om tatsa... Om dhiyo...
   prachodayat.
   The japa endows the worshipper with high
   spiritual power.
4. The following japa is called *panchapada* because
   five 'Om's are affixed.
   Om bhuh Om bhuvah Om svah
   Om tatsa.... dhimahi ˘
   Om dhiyo ... prachodayat ˘
   The mantra is believed to cure cardiac problems.
5. The following japa is called *shatpada* since it
   involves six pranavas.
   Om bhuh Om bhuvah Om svah˘
   Om tatsaviturvarenyam Om bhargo ... dhimahi˘
   Om dhiyo... prachodayat˘
   The mantra is said to cure problems relating to
   blood pressure and asthma.
6. In *Narada Purana* four additional vyahritis are
   prescribed. They are mahah, janah, tapah and
   satyam.
7. Om is also used in creating an extended Gayatri.
   At the end of the Gayatri the following sheersha
   of Gayatri japa appears :
   Om apo jyoti rasomritam ˘
   Brahma bhurbhuvahsvarom˘
8. A hundred-letter (*shatakshara*) Gayatri is
   composed as follows: To the 'ekapada' (p. 92) the
   following is added.
   (a) Om jatavedase sunavam somamarati yato
       nidahati Vedah/Sa nah parshadati Durgani
       vishva naveva Sindhum Duritatyagnih.
   (b) Om Tryambakam yajamahe sugandhim
       pushtivardhanam/Urvarukamiva bandhanat
       mrityormrikshiya mamritat.

The Gayatri japa averts untimely death as well as physical and mental suffering.

9. *Amritasanjivani Gayatri* reads as:

> Om bhurbhuvah svah Om
> Tryambakam yajamahe˘ Om
> tatsaviturvarenyam ˘ Sugandhim
> pushtivardhanam ˘Bhargodevasya
> dhimahi˘
> Urvarukamiva bandhanat ˘Dhiyo yo
> nah prachodayat ˘Mrityormukshiya
> mamritat ˘Om˘

You will find that the elements of the gayatri are interspersed with Om and other mantras.

The mantra is used to avert untimely death.

10. In the *tri-pranava gayatri* Om appears thrice

> Om Bhurbhuvahsvah ˘ Om
> tatsaviturvarenyam ˘
> Bhargodevasyadhimahi dhiyo yo nah
> prachodayat Om˘

In this and most other modified Gayatris you will find that the Gayatri is broken into components and fillers like Om or other mantras are used to create a new and longer mantra. This aspect will be discussed in chapter 15.

The etymology of *vyahriti* is vi+a+hrati which means pronunciation or japa. The vyahritis are believed to have a close relationship with peace (shanti) according to some mantras.

The Gayatris of other Deities

The Gayatri discussed above is the Savitragayatri. Many more gayatris have been created in honour of other

devatas. Om is invariably prefixed to all these gayatris.
For example, Shri Ganesha gayatri appears as:

Om ekadantaya vidmahe Vakratundaya dhimahi
Tanno dantih prachodayat.

It seems Om is inseparable from the gayatris. The
other gayatris having similar constructions as above
have been composed to honour the following deities.
Each gayatri starts with Om.

Shiva, Vishnu, Sarasvati, Krishna, Agni, Aditya,
Hanumana, Rama, Surya (Sun), Yama (god of death),
Varuna, Shanmukha, Hamsa, Durga, Mahalakshmi,
Gauri, Guru, Narasimha, Radha, Ganesha, etc. Each deity
is worshipped for specific purposes. For instance,
Ganesha for intelligence, Hanumana for physical strength,
Hamsa for renunciation of worldly pleasures etc.

What is surprising is that the gayatris have been
composed even in honour of saints such as Swami
Samartha, a 17th century ascetic, Sai Baba a 19th century
saint etc.

Since Om is prefixed, suffixed or infixed in all gayatris,
Om is obviously treated as a magical symbol which
would enhance the value of other mantras.

The connection between Om and the Gayatri is much
deeper than mere affixation of Om in the Gayatri
mantra. We recall that there were several meanings of
the matras A-U-M of Om. You will remember that one
of the interpretations is A(bhuh - earth), U (bhuvah -
sky), and M (svah - heaven) which refer to the three
vyahritis. These vyahritis in turn have been interpreted
in terms of the other meanings of A, U, M.

Incidentally, the vyahritis mahah, janah, tapah,
satyam are interpreted as Supreme Being (also the half
matra of Om), primal cause, brilliance par excellence
and truth respectively.

We may also mention the Savitrimantra of the Gupta sect, which has elements of the Gayatri coupled with Om.

Om   bhuh   Savitri   pravishami   ˇOm tatsaviturvarenyam (Vishvamitra)
Om bhuvah Savitri pravishami ˇBhargodevasya dhimahi (Gayatri meter)
Om svah Savitri pravishami ˇDhiyo yo nah prachodayat Om ˇ(Savita Devata)

Gayatri is not just a meter, she is treated as a goddess. "Gayanatam trayate Gayatri" 'Gaya' means prana and Gayatri is the devata that protects life-force. It appears that what was originally a meter was elevated to the position of deity and its close association with Om makes the Gayatri none other than Brahman.

An interesting connection between Om, Brahman, Gayatri and vyahritis is mentioned by Swami Sarvananda. Om is said to be the acoustic symbol of Brahman and also the first sound produced at the time of the Creation. From the three matras of Om, emanated the 'feet' of Gayatri and from these three feet, arose the the first three Vedas and the three worlds earth, sky, heaven corresponding to bhuh bhuvah svah. From A of AUM arose 'tat savitur varenyam' which became the Rigveda. From U emanated 'bhargo devasya dhimahi' which expanded itself into the Yajurveda, and from M arose 'dhiyo yo nah prachodayat' which amplified into the Sama Veda. The first is hymnal (*stutipara*), the second is devoted to work (*kriyapara*) and the third pertains to knowledge (*jnanapara*).

While meditation upon different matras leads to the benefits mentioned above, Brahman can only be realised when the mind is concentrated on the inaudible ardhamatra.

Ten

MANTRAS AND MANTRASHASTRA

"Hreem streem hoom hoom streem
streem hoom hoom streem hreem."
- A mantra used in ritual for the success of a project.

Since Om is considered the most sacred mantra, it would be instructive to say a few words about mantras and mantrashastra (*shastra* means a body of knowledge or science).

We have already discussed the theory of sound according to Mimamsa where it was mentioned that Om is the primordial sound from which other sounds and letters were created. This implies that Om is also the source of all mantras.

Etymologically, 'mantra' means an instrument to think. A mantra is treated as an utterance that has the power to protect. But we shall see that mantras are used for a variety of purposes, some of them destructive. What's more, most mantras used for constructive or destructive purposes consider Om as a potent weapon which increases the strength of the mantra.

Types of Mantras

Brahmanda Purana lists nine *vidhis* (methods) relating to Vedic mantras. It also lists twenty-four kinds which include praise, criticism, question etc.

Maha vakyas ('great sentences') are aphorisms from Upanishads and are usually related to Vedanta. We have already considered them in relation to the identity of the Self and Brahman. Another well-known maha vakya, Soham, which is believed to incorporate Om, has already been discussed at length in chapter 1.

Mahamantras are those powerful mantras which are not found in texts but are passed down from the guru to his disciple. They have an aura of secrecy and are to be used for Self-realisation under the guidance of the teacher.

Apta mantras are ordinary words which have great power. They are not formally taught but are to be picked up by those who can appreciate their power.

Siddha mantras are those which are believed to bestow siddhis or supernatural powers. Tantra texts describe many such mantras.

Shabar mantras are mantras believed to be created for the benefit of the ordinary people by Shiva. They appear strange and unintelligible and are used for curing diseases and for earthly gains not only in India but also in South East Asia, China and Tibet.

Mantras have also been classified according to their gender. For instance the masculine mantras end with *vashat* or *phat*. Those which terminate with *voshat* are feminine and the mantras ending with *namah* have neuter gender.

Bija Mantras

Mantras have been classified on the basis of the number of syllables they contain. According to *Nitya Tantra*, those mantras which contain upto ten syllables are called *mulamantras* or *bijamantras*, those having more than ten but less than twenty syllables are called *kartari mantras* and those having in excess of twenty syllables are termed *mala mantras*.

For us, bija mantras are the most important. They are usually monosyllabic and nasalised. Bija means 'seed'. All bijas are believed to convey some meaning—though most of the bijas are not listed in ordinary dictionaries. Om or pranava is the most important bija and is called adibija (first seed) from which other bijas have sprouted.

To distinguish between one bija and another which are transliterated identically in English, we will have to use a slightly modified phonetic way of spelling. We give below the Devanagari alphabet (Romanised) in which Sanskrit and many Indian languages are written,

Vowels:

a	aa	i	ee	u	oo	*ri*
ree	*li*	*lee*	e			
ai	o	au	am (*anusvara*)	ah (*visarga*)		

Consonants:

k	kh	g	gh	n
ch	chh	j	jh	n'
t	*th*	*d*	*dh*	*n*
t	th	d	dh	n
p	ph	b	bh	m
y	r	l	v	sh
sh	s	h		

The vowels are pronounced as follows :

a(f*u*n), aa (*a*rm), i(*i*n), ee(m*ee*t), u (p*u*t), oo (f*oo*d), *ri* (short retroflex vowel slightly resembling the third syllable in ability, *ree* is longer *ri*; *li* is a vowel resembling lry in revelry); *lee* is longer *li*; ai(*ai*sle), o (n*o*), au (c*ow*), am (nasalisation of 'a'). A consonant can also be nasalised: kam, kim etc., 'ah' (slightly aspirated 'a'); *t*, *d*, are retroflex t, d, ... etc., in which the tongue is curled backwards. A consonant followed by h indicates aspiration of the consonant for instance, kh (work*h*ouse)

Sh is retroflex sh; **n** (si*n*g), *n* (a*n*d) n'(as in ni*n*a, girl child in Spanish); 'm' is as in English, but also used for nasalisation. All other consonants are pronounced approximately as in English.[1] A few letters are omitted to avoid complications. Note that this phonetic plan will be used only for the bijas; especially when two bijas having slightly different sounds are juxtaposed (such as; am, aam). The scheme will be found useful in the chapter on tantra.

Some bijas with their significance are listed below:

Om - pranava, 'tar', Brahman, primordial sound, the first bija (adibija)

aam - Ananta or infinite, Vinayaka or Ganesha

im - Chandra or moon, Rudra, Ganesha as the remover of obstacles.

em - Sarasvati or speech

eem - Gayatri, Lakshmi, Mother Veda

kam - Mahakali

kham - Akasha (sky) and also Brahman

gam - Ganges, Ganesha

pam - Shani or saturn

yam - Vayu

ram - Agni or fire

lam - Amrita or elixir, earth, corpse

sham - kama (sex, passion)

ham - Shiva

hreem - Girija (goddess)

streem - woman

kleem - kama (sex, passion)

shreem - universe (vishva)
haum - Shiva, prasada
glaum - earth, Ganesha
Strictly speaking, we must distinguish between Om (AUM) which is the primordial bija and om (nasalisation of 'O') which indicates Gayatri trayodashi (13th day of the Hindu calendar), Trailokyavijaya (the goddess conquering three worlds) etc.

Bija mantras are also believed to have specific powers. For example, 'vashat' is used at the end of a mantra to influence people. *Phat* destroys enemies, *namah* is used for gaining god's favour. *Vaushat* is used to acquire wealth.

Bijas are classified according to the varnas of the practitioners. For example, *rheem* is to be used by brahmins, *sreem* by kshatriyas, *kleem* by vaishyas and *em* by shudras.

While Om is the most sacred symbol, when added to other mantras the latter appear to be more potent.

For example, "Om gam", Om bhuvah svah, Om hreem gam, Om gam. In Shakti-Vinayaka Ganapati mantra the following combinations of bijas appear:

Om graam, Om greem, Om groom, Om graim, Om graum, Om grah
In another mantra related to goddess Gauri and Ganapati 'Om gam' appears several times, The following combinations too appear : Om kleem, Om glaum, Om pam.

A zodiac sign is associated with a mantra solely consisting of bijas in which Om precedes all.
Aries (Mesha) - Om, aim, kleem, saum
Taurus (Vrishabha) - Om hreem, kleem, sreem
Gemini (Mithuna) - Om, sreem, aim, sau

Cancer(Karka) - Om, aim, kleem, sreem
Leo (Simha) - Om, hreem, sreem, sau
Virgo (Kanya) - Om, sreem, aim, sau
Libra (Tula) - Om hreem, kleem, sreem
Scorpio (Vrishchika) - Om, aim, kleem, sau
Sagittarius (Dhanu) - Om, hreem, kleem, sau
Capricorn (Makara) - Om, aim, kleem, hreem, sreem, sau
Aquarius - (Kumbha) - Om, hreem, aim, hreem kleem, sreem
Piesces (Mina) - Om, hreem, kleem, sau

Since mantras have putative powers which may be beneficial or harmful, we may think that there are two mutually exclusive kinds of mantras that are either constructive or destructive.

The following is the list of a few 'good' bijas:

Bija	Nature	Benefit
Om	pranava, Brahman	liberation
sreem	Lakshmi	wealth
aim	Sarasvati	knowledge

These bijas are 'compounded' (*samput*) with other specific mantras. But consider the following 'saptashati' bijas and their effects.

Dislodgement and destruction - Om phrom, aim, hreem, sreem

Influence and seduction - Om hreem aim hreem ghreem

Jealousy - Om phrem, phrom, aim, ai hreem shreem

Killing or destroying - Om krom, hum, phat aim, hreem, sreem

It will be found that the bijas which are considered benevolent become malevolent either alone or in a group of bijas. The most startling example is the ubiquitous Om which is used both in constructive and destructive mantras. Om in this case seems to be considered a catalyst which increases the power of mantras rather than a holy symbol. Similar is the case of other benevolent mantras like shreem or aim. It is extremely difficult to formulate the chemistry of combination of bijas. A way to avoid this is to consider a syntactic (structural) approach to mantras and rituals rather than the semantic method. This is briefly discussed in a later chapter.

Mudras

Mudras ('seals') are gestures which are used in conjuction with mantras and yantras (geometrical figures) in many religious ceremonies, and also in yoga and tantra.

Different mudras are used to seek favour from various deities. For example, 29 mudras are used in the worship of Gayatri. There are mudras to be performed before a puja (worship), at the time of invocation and after the puja.

The most important mudras used in a puja are *surabhi* (fabulous cow of plenty), *jnanam* (wisdom, knowledge), vairagyam (asceticism), yoni (female reproductive organ), shankha (conch), pankajam (lotus), lingam (phallus) and nirvanam (liberation). Since a puja is always interspersed with Om, the association of pranava with mudras in puja is very intimate.

In yoga and tantra, mudras are used for specific purposes. For example, *maha mudra* (great mudra) described in *Hatha Yoga Pradipika* is believed to cure leprosy, piles and many other ailments. It is also said to destroy death and pain.

Nyasa

Nyasa is a technique in which different parts of mantras are synchronised or 'deposited' on the various parts of the body.

Karanyasa is the nyasa related to the hand. For example, in the tantric method of worshipping Gayatri, the Gayatri mantra is broken into six parts each of four syllables. These parts are then 'deposited' on thumbs, the index fingers, middle fingers, ring fingers and the palms. At the time of synchronising, Om and the name of the body part are interspersed. For example, the nyasa related to the thumb appears as :

Om bhuh bhuvah svah tat savituh
Om bhuh bhuvah svah angushthabhyam namah
(*angushthabhyam* refers to the thumb).

Anganyasa is similar to karanyasa. In the Gayatri worship, for example, the parts of the body that are syncronised with the Gayatri elements are the heart, head, crown of the head, chest and shoulders, eyes and the space occupied by the pranic body. In addition to Om which appears in every line of the mantras, other bijas like hum, vaushat, etc., also appear.

Prana Pratishtha

This is a process which establishes the life-force (prana) into an idol. Before starting the main puja or ceremony, the deity is invoked. Placing the palms over the heart the worshipper meditates on the deity, reciting tantric or Vedic mantras. For example, in the tantric method of worshipping Gayatri, the mantra appears as a cluster of bijas interspersed with other words.

Om am hrim krim yam ram lam vam sham *sham*
sam ham hamsah soham mama hridaye bhagavati

gayatri ihaivagtya sukham chiram tishthatu svaha.
Om Om Om pratistha.

You will appreciate the importance of Om and other
bijas in nyasa as well as in prana pratishtha.

Mantra Shastra

The word *shastra* in the broadest sense means a body of
knowledge. However, for those who use this word, it
has a connotation which is beyond the mere study of
mantras. They believe that mantra shastra is a science
which can be used for various purposes : fulfillment of
earthly wishes or acquisition of supernatural powers.
We may say that mantra shastra uses mantras and
rituals as tools to bring about the desired results.

There was no separate discipline called mantra
shastra because the Atharvaveda was regarded as the
repository of mantras and rituals to be used for desired
effects.

The *Gopatha Brahmana* describes the application of the
Atharva mantras and rituals in five kinds of suktas. A
brief summary of the topics covered is furnished below:

Kaushikasutra—weaponary, cure of many diseases,
exorcism, agriculture, navigation, expiation of sin.

Nakshatrakalpa—'protection rituals', weaponary
including missiles, fulfillment of wishes, seismology.

Vaitana Sankalpa—Several yajnas like Vajapeya,
Ashvamedha etc. for yielding specific results.

Angirasakalpa—Several mantras for specific deities,
Ganesha, Lakshmi etc.

Shantikalpa - 'Shanti' means peace and a shanti ritual
is performed to avoid the wrath of gods and planets.

In addition to the Atharva there are hundreds of tantra
texts and the treatises which are used as the sources of
mantra shastra.

We must mention a special type of weapons called 'astras' in which the fuel used was neither petrol nor electricity but 'mantras'. Mantras when chanted properly and at the right time were believed to garner the universal forces to have the desired effects.

If your adversary launched an agni-astra (fire missile) you could retaliate with a *prajanya-astra* which would create rainfall and extinguish the fire.

Needless to say, Om played an important role in mantrashastra. As mentioned, earlier, Om could be regarded as a magical syllable that could accelerate the process of wish fulfillment.

If we include yoga and tantra in mantra shastra, the scope of mantrashastra can then be divided into the following categories.

1. *Psychophysiological changes*—These include a sense of well being, peace of mind, ecstasy, heavenly bliss etc.

Some of these claims can be tested. For example, if Om or 'Om shantih shantih shantih' is the japa that is prescribed for peace of mind, it may lead to the state of relaxation.

It has been proved that such psychophysical changes do take place in hypnosis, suggestion or psychotherapy. Faith also seems to play a role in the effect of mantras. Experiments conducted confirm that in some cases even diseases can be cured or their exacerbation arrested. The reason seems to be based on the unity of the body-mind complex which is open to suggestion.

2. *Transcendental Effects*—These include liberation from the cycle of birth and death, a place in heaven, meeting gods, rebirth etc.

This category belongs to what may be called non-science because these claims cannot be refuted. We need not discuss this topic, but leave it to the individual's faith and belief.

3. *Miracles* - Miracles are events which exceed the known powers of nature and are attributable to supernatural powers and siddhis. They include levitation, travelling to other planets with mantras, knowing the past and the future, ability to effect changes from distance etc. They also include ESP and psychokinesis which were the subject of experimentation in many universities a few decades ago.

We may say from the evidence available so far that miracles or the possession of supernatual powers have not yet been proved scientifically under controlled conditions.

Nevertheless, a few mantras are given below which are used for various purposes by those who believe in mantrashastra.

1. For acquiring wealth - 'Om kleem rheem' to be recited one million times along with a longer mantra.
2. For controlling flora - Om namo jaya bhagavati matre Durgayai namah.
3. For destroying enemies - 'Om joom chham joom chham joom chheem, joom, chhaum, joom chhah' with other rituals.
4. For the celestial cow (kamadhenu) to appear before you, 'Om rheem sreem Om kamadurge prasphur prasphur Om' along with other rituals.
5. For becoming invisible 'Aim srim Om ksham' (108 times)

6. To see any object you wish to—'Om jvala jvala prajvala sphur sphur prasphur prasphur Indrajaliko devata Aum hum phat Om tham tham tham'
7. For acquiring lost wealth—'Om aivam devya varam labdhva... namah.'

Most of the mantras are to be recited with ancillary rites which may involve yantras.

Note the use of Om to facilitate miracles. Note also the preponderance of bijas.

Om and Planets

In the ancient Indian tradition there were nine planets viz. the Sun, Moon, Mars, Venus, Jupiter, Mercury, Saturn, Rahu, Ketu. These planets are treated as gods and worshipped or propitiated.

In Indian astrology these planets have an important place. They are believed to influence not only the elements of the earth including flora and fauna but also determine our destiny. The worship of these planets includes mantras, yantras and other rituals as well as charms and precious stones. The planets may be worshipped to acquire special powers which they are believed to possess and bestow, or to appease them if their influence is perceived to be harmful to a particular individual. The Vedas, Puranas and tantra constitute the major sources of rituals and mantras used for this purpose. Our interest is of course confined to Om. It is interesting to find that in the bija mantras or japa mantras which are to be recited several times, Om finds a prominent place in the Vedic and tantric sources. The following table shows how important is pranava for those who worship the planets.

Planet	Bija or Japa mantra (Vedic)	Bija or Japa mantra (Tantric)
Sun (Surya)	Om hraam hreem sah Suryaya namah	Om shree Suryaya Svaha
Moon (Chandra)	Om Chandram Chandraya namah	Om Chandram Chandraya namah
Mars (Mangala)	Om kraam kreem kaum sah Bhumaya namah	Om haam ham sah kham khah
Mercury (Budha)	Om bram breem braum sah Bhudaya namah	Om jraam jreem jraum sah
Jupiter (Guru)	Om gram greem graum sah Guruve namah	Brim Brihaspataye namah
Venus (Shukra)	Om draam dreem draum sah Shukraya namah	Shum Shukrayam namah svaha
Saturn (Shani)	Om shreem shreem shroom Shanaishwaraya namah	Shum Shanaishvara namah
- (Rahu)	Om bhraam bhreem	Om bhraam bhreem

	bhraum sah	bhraum sah
	Rahave	Rahave namah
- (Ketu)	Om straam	Om shram
	streem	shreem
	straum sah	shaum Ketave
	Ketave namah	namah

Eleven

TANTRA

"Om namah Shivaya"
(Om, obeisance to Lord Shiva)

A popular refrain, also inscribed in a yantra tantriks use in Sri Vidya worship. It is believed to be efficacious only when written in the Devanagari script.

"*Vashat* for manipulating, *phat* for creating frustration, *hum* for creating animosity and hatred, *khem* for killing. *Svaha* for gaining favour, *namah* for acquiring blessings and health, *vaushat* for wealth."

A well-known verse in tantra indicating the uses of certain bija mantras.

'Tantra' means weaving. It is believed that all of us are born with a natural pattern designed by Mother Nature. However, because of our defect in life-style the harmony of the pattern with nature is disturbed. Tantra 'reweaves' this fabric. Tantra is usually regarded as an unorthodox system for acquiring power (siddhi) and liberation, because it employs some methods alien to the traditional Vedic heritage. It has many schools and is practised in Hinduism as well as Buddhism.

From our standpoint tantra is no less important than other modes of worship involving pranava. The importance of Om is supreme in tantra because not only is pranava considered sacred, it is in this discipline that we find extensive use of other bijas which are believed to emanate from Om. There are also innumerable yantras used in tantra which makes this mode of sadhana unique. No other spiritual system has evoked as much awe and fear as tantra which has a mystical aura.

Tantra regards the human body as a microcosm containing diverse parts of the universe. With meditation and other rituals tantra awakens the internal forces to harness the power corresponding to the macrocosm. However, tantric practice needs to be undertaken under the guidance of a competent teacher.

Tantriks worship goddess Shakti (power) who is contrasted with Shiva the masculine universal consciousness. There is a tantric principle according to which only gods can worship a god. You will recall that according to one theory of sound, a sound pattern is associated with a deity. This mantra-deity duo is used to divinise the worshippers who can identify themselves with specific gods and goddesses.

There are many schools of tantra which were once practised not only in India but also in China, Afghanistan, Tibet and Java (Indonesia).

Today most tantric shrines in India are situated in the North and North-East. A shrine also exists in Malabar Hills in Kerala.

There are many types of tantras and tantra texts which gave rise to numerous tantra schools. A tantra text is usually in the form of a dialogue between Shiva and Parvati. Those tantras narrated by Shiva to Parvati are called *agama* and those in which Parvati was the narrator are called *nigama*. However, the word nigama is also used to indicate the Vedas.

Some of the most famous tantras once practised in differen regions are:

Siddhishvara, Kalitantra, Nilatantra, Kularnava, Yoginitantra, Brahmayamala, Rudrayamala, Kubjikatantra Sabaratantra Damaratantra, Varahitantra, Indrajala, Kundalinitantra, Bhutashuddhi, Mohanatantra and Mahanirvanatantra. Nearly 256 tantras have been summarised in the text *Sarvatantrasvatantra*. There is a belief that Ganesha is incessantly creating new tantras and yantras on Mt. Kailash.

We shall follow Pandit Rajamani Tigunait according to whom a broad classification of tantra is (1) *Kaula* which can be practised by householders, (2) *Samaya* which lays emphasis on meditation, and (3) *Mishra* which is a blend of the two schools.

The Chakra System

Tantra and to some extent Yoga have an esoteric system of anatomy and physiology: there is a correspondence between (1) the parts of the body, (2) mantras, (3) yantras, and (4) the letters of the alphabet.

Nadis are the currents of energy. There are about 72,000 nadis. A junction of two nadis is called *sandhi* and an intersection of three nadis is *marma sthana*. The point where more than three nadis meet is called *chakra*. The centre of each chakra is associated with a characteristic sound.

The central channel of energy is called *sushumna* which links the anus or the base of the spine with the crown of the head. The channel on the left of the sushumna is *ida* and that on the right is *pingala*. The energy in ida is called 'blue dot' or *asita bindu*. The energy in pingala is 'red hot' or *rakta bindu*. The currents of energy in different channels interact with these bindus giving rise to countless patterns of vibrations.

The major chakras are located along the axis of sushumna. They are (1) *muladhara* near anus, (2) *svadhishthana* near regenerative organs, (3) *manipura* at the navel, (4) *anahata* in the region of heart, (5) *vishuddha* at the throat, and (6) *ajna* between the eyes. At the crown lies the 'thousand petalled' *sahasrara* which is not usually called a chakra. Each chakra or lotus has a specific number of petals which are associated with different bijas. Every chakra also has a bijamantra at the centre. All these bijas are nasalised monosyllables originating from Om. A god and goddess (different forms of Shakti) are also associated with each chakra. A brief description of the chakras is given below. It should be noted that scholars differ sometimes in respect of various aspects of the chakra.

These chakras are also called lotuses with petals.

Muladhara

1. Location—Spinal centre of region below genitals.
2. Central Bija—lam on Airavata (elephant).
3. Petals—4, red with unpleasent smell.
4. Bijas emanating from petals—vam, sham, *sh*am, sam (clockwise).
5. Regnant tattava and its qualities—Earth, cohesion; stimulates sense of smell.
6. God—Bala (child) Brahma on Hamsa.
7. Goddess (shakti)—Dakini.
8. Linga and yoni—Svayambhu and Tripura trikona (triangle).
9. Mandala ('circuit')—Square

This chakra is the base which supports all other chakras. The sun is believed to reside where the linga and yoni are located. Around the linga is the serpent-like kundalini (shakti) coiled three and a half times. Under normal conditions, the kundalini is dormant.

It will be recalled that we mentioned in chapter 6 that the muladhara is also the abode of Ganesha. Note also that the vahana of the central bija is a celestial elephant.

Svadhishtana

1. Location—Spinal centre of region above genitals
2. Central Bija—vam on Makara
3. Petals—6, Vermillion colour, bad odor
4. Petal bijas—*ba*m, bham, mam, yam, ram, lam (clockwise)
5. Tattva /Stimulation—water, contraction, sense of taste
6. God—Vishnu on Garuda
7. Goddess—Rakini
8. Linga and yoni— —
9. Mandala—Crescent

Manipura

1. Location—Spinal centre of the navel.
2. Central bija—ram on a ram
3. Petals—10,
4. Petal bijas—*da*m, *dha*m, *na*m, tam, tham, dam, dham, nam, pam, pham
5. Tattva /stimulation—Brilliance, expansion, heat, sense of colour and form.
6. God—Rudra on a bull
7. Goddess—Lakini
8. Linga and yoni— —
9. Mandala—Triangle

Anahata

1. Location—Spinal centre of region of the heart.
2. Central bija—yam on an antelope

3. Petals—12
4. Petal bijas—kam, kham, gam, gham, nam, (clockwise), cham, chham, jam, jham, n'am, tam, tham.
5. Tattva /stimalation—Air movement, sense of touch
6. God—Pinaki (Isha)
7. Goddess—Kakini
8. Linga and yoni—Bana and trikona
9. Mandala—Six-pointed hexagon

This is the chakra of 'unstruck sound' identified with Om.

Vishuddha

1. Location—Spinal center of region of the throat
2. Central bija—ham on a white elephant
3. Petals—16
4. Petal bijas —(clockwise) am, aam, im, eem, um, oom, rim, reem, lim, leem, em, aim, om, aum, am, ah
5. Tattva /stimulation—Ether, space, sense of hearing
6. God—Sadashiva
7. Goddess—Sakini
8. Linga and yoni—   —
9. Mandala—Circle

Ajna

1. Location—Centre of region between the eyebrows
2. Central bija—Om
3. Petals—2
4. Petal bijas—(clockwise) ksham, hum

5. Tattva /stimulation—Mental faculties
6. God—Shambhu
7. Goddess—Hakini
8. Linga and yoni—Itara and trikona
9. Mandala—Half Shiva

Sahasrara — At the crown of the head lies sahasrara, the thousand petalled lotus. It is whiter than the full moon. Within it is the cool moon shedding its rays. Inside it is *A - kathadi triangle* in which there is *Para bindu, Great void or Shunya.* This Shunya is hidden and is the root of liberation. Here is Brahman or Parama Shiva and Atman of all. According to *Shiva Samhita,* a holier place than the sahasrara does not exist.

Awakening Kundalini

There are many tantric methods of awakening the kundalini which is otherwise dormant. The kundalini rises and breaks through the several chakras. It ultimately reaches the sahasrara. When Devi Kundalini reaches Para Shiva's abode, she drinks nectar and the worshipper is liberated and merges with the Supreme Shakti. The kundalini then returns to her original place viz. muladhara. Many schools treat the body as yantra and ask the students to successively meditate on the chakras from the muladhara upwards. In the Samaya school, the sadhaka meditates on the sahasrara.

Ganesha or Om in Tantra

In chapter 6 we mentioned several qualities of Ganesha and its identification with Om and Brahman. Tantriks, especially those who follow the kaula school, regard Ganesha as an extremely important deity in their worship.

Ganesha is called the gatekeeper of the Divine Mother's palace. When the sadhaka meditates properly, it is Ganapati who stimulates the muladhara where the most subtle sound rests in the para state. This vibrationless sound rises to the navel and can be felt by the worshipper. The sound incorporates the power of thinking when it reaches the anahata. It becomes audible when it reaches the vishuddha chakra. The process is overseen by Ganesha who is also the lord of gravity, and the movement against gravity is possible only through his permission.

Tantriks believe that Ganesha with his huge body and small feet dances to the song of Mother Shakti. Both the mother and the son perform the cosmic dance which is responsible for awakening the kundalini. It is Ganesha who bestows on the sadhaka divine energy. He is also responsible for sending the proper master (*sat guru*) to guide us. Without Ganesha it is not possible even to enter his abode, the muladhara, let alone the palace of Divine Mother.

Ganesha is propitiated in several ways by meditation, usually in conjunction with yantra sadhana.

The Ganesha yantra has a circle at the centre surrounded by three circuits. Ganesha rests at the centre seated on his vahana—mouse. Shankaracharya in his *Prapancha Sara* describes the yantra in detail.

According to him the mouse though small is a union or manifestation of nine forces or powers viz. intensity (*tivra*), radiance (*jvalini*), delight (*nanda*), pleasure (*bhogada*), desire (*kamarupini*), speed (*ugra*), illumination (*tejovati*), being or existence (*satya*), destruction of resistance (*vighna vinashini*). All these forces constitute what is called *pitha shakti*, i.e. the power of Ganesh's seat.

His two intrinsic powers, intelligence (*buddhi*) and success (*siddhi*) are always with him on the left and on his right. Ganesha himself symbolises the static part while buddhi and siddhi are dynamic parts that originate in him.

The first circuit of the yantra is represented by a square in which reside static and dynamic powers (shaktis) radiating from Ganapati.

North—Lakshmi and Vishnu   (sustenance)
East—Varaha (Boar) and   (stability)
        Mahi (Earth)
South—Shiva and Shakti   (reconstruction)
West—Kamadeva and Rati   (love and attraction)

Each pair has different functions and all shaktis are controlled and coordinated by Ganesha. Through them Ganesha maintains the entire universe.

The six-petalled flower forms the second circuit. The six pairs of static and dynamic powers (shaktis) inhabiting these petals are:

1. Amoda and Riddhi (earthly and spiritual riches).
2. Pramoda and Samriddhi (earthly and spiritual enjoyment).
3. Avighnesha and Madadrava (intoxication, ecstacy).
4. Durmukha and Madanavati (craving and indulgence).
5. Vighnakarta and Dravani (liquefaction).
6. Sumukha and Kanti (beautification).

It is necessary to know that these different pairs have good as well as bad aspects. Unless these various shaktis are used in a proper mix one would not lead a balanced life. It is Ganesha who from the centre controls and coordinates these forces to maintain the equilibrium.

To illustrate how these powers need to be coordinated consider the first pair which gives riches. You will not be able to use these assets unless you know how to enjoy them. The second pair precisely performs this function. The third pair is believed to help you empathise with others and share their joy. The fourth pair makes us avaracious and vainglorious.

The fifth pair gives us elation when we find others are in trouble. Coupled with the fourth pair, these forces can be a source of obstacles. The third pair has a shakti Avighnesha (remover of obstacles) while the fifth has vighnakarta (creator of obstacles). Unless the former counterbalances the latter, we would be treading a treacherous path. The sixth shakti represents our inner beauty and strength. Sumukha, for example, means the beautiful- faced in contrast to Durmukha (fourth pair) or the evil-faced. You will appreciate that this circuit contains opposite tendencies, and tantriks believe that it is only with the blessings of Ganesha that all these shaktis can be so directed that we lead a happy life in the long run despite the short-term gains and losses.

The third or the outermost circuit is a circle which contains the following static and dynamic pairs of shaktis.

1. Shankhanidhi and Vasundhara which keep our inner and outer assets moving.
2. Padmanidhi and Vasumati which stabilize these assets or wealth.

These opposing shaktis which represent flux and stability must work in coordination. Without flux we would stagnate and without stability we would disintegrate.

The sadhaka has to 'enter' the Ganesha yantra under the guidence of a teacher who prescribes specific mantras and meditation on the specific parts of the yantra. If you are successful in 'reaching' the centre of the yantra where Ganesha or Om resides, you become physically, mentally and spiritually much stronger than what you were. It will be recalled that Ganesha resides in the muladhara chakra and controls your physical, emotional and intellectual health.

After you are repeatedly tested by your teacher, he may decide that you are ready to undertake any tantric sadhana. The right-hand kaula or *dakshinmarga* involves advanced worship of yantra which includes contemplation, visualisation, recitation of mantras and other yajna- like rituals. The right-hand kaula believes in puritan views, austerities, and avoids liquor, meat, fish and sex.

The left-hand kaula or vam marga is unorthodox, but its practitioners consider it as more advanced. If you have not gone through this stage you have missed the highest echelons of tantra.

In the left-hand (vama marga) kaula which involves chakra puja, the body is treated as a living yantra. Those who practice the vama marga use five 'M's : wine (*madya*), meat (*mamsa*), fish (*matsya*), gestures (*mudras*), sex (*maithuna*) which are called *panchamakara*.

The vama margis maintain that the gulf between the sacred and the profane can be bridged only by boldly facing your primitive urges and mastering the instincts rather than running away from them. We shall not describe the sadhana involved. Suffice it to point out that it involves invocation of the indispensable Ganesha, Om and other sages, and worshipping Mother Goddess. At the end of the practice if the worshipper is successful, he merges with Mother Shakti and dissolves in her.

There are a few ancillary modes of rituals and worship which accompany tantric worship. For example, prana pratishtha, nyasa, and japa constitute the initial course given to the sadhaka. In prana pratishtha the sadhaka meditates on the anahata chakra. Nyasa involves depositing the Gayatri elements on several parts of the body in which Om is used for affixation.

Yantras

Yantras are geometrical figures used in tantra. We have already mentioned the duo deity-mantra. Tantriks believe that a yantra is associated with a deity and a mantra. We should speak, therefore, of the triplets deity-mantra-yantra emanating from the Supreme Being. It must however, be mentioned that more than one yantra may be associated with a given deity.

Hundreds of yantras are described in literature. They are not only used for the kundalini yoga whose primary purpose is merging with the Supreme Being, but also for mundane purposes, as vehicles for wish fulfilment.

Sri Yantra is perhaps the most revered yantra symbolising goddess Sri Devi or Shodashi. It is believed to incorporate all other yantras. Yantras may have different shapes, and are made of the material according to specific rules. One can perceive different types of symmetry in the yantras. This aspect has been described in this author's *Rituals, Mantras and Science.*

Yantras are used for specific purposes. Hanumana yantra is used as an antidote for ill health, loss of wealth and family feuds. Dhanayasha prapti yantra is worshipped every day for prosperity and is made of copper. The renowned Sri yantra is used for prosperity of the family. Sri Bagalmukhi yantra is used for inflicting injury(*marana*), frustrating enemies (*uchhatana*), propitiating planets, seduction (*vashikarana*) and many other purposes. Sri Mahamrityunjaya yantra is used for curing diseases, for wealth and prosperity. These yantras are usually used in association with ancillary rituals.

In addition to geometrical patterns yantras may have inscriptions, either numerical or verbal. Our interest lies in the latter. Most of such yantras contain Om or other bijas emanating from it. They may also contain the names of the deities and other mantras. The following brief list will give you an idea of the preponderence of Om and allied bijas.

Yantra	Inscribed bijas [Bracketed figures indicate the no. of the bijas on one yantra.]
Gita	Om (13)
Sri Krishna	Om (2), Shree (4)
Siddha Ganesha	Om, gam (2), hum (3), Shreem (many)
Sri Datta	Shreem (3), kleem (2), *aa*m (1), hreem (1)
Sri Datta	Om (5), dram (1), hreem (1), kleem (1)
Rama	Om (central), shreem (1), hreem (1), kleem (1)
Rama	Om (8)
Vanadurga	Om (central), many other bijas
Shiva	Om (central), Om (2)
Shiva	Om (2), numerals

Surya (sun)	Om (central), hreem (central)
Sri Yantra (wealth)	Om, kleem, shreem, hreem
Sri Yantra (numerical)	hreem and numerals
Bhagvati	Om (central), hreem, kleem, shreem
Sri Krishna	Om (central), Om, shreem (4)
Mata Svapnavali (wealth)	hreem (7)
Gayatri	Om (central), Om (3)
Dhanada (wealth)	Om (4)
Sri Hanuman	hreem (2), Om (8)

Needless to say, Om reigns supreme in most yantras. It is also necessary to remember that other bijas stem from Om.

Sri Vidya

Our discussion on tantra will not be complete unless we say at least a few words about Sri Vidya. Sri Vidya is considered an incomprehensible mystery. It is believed to encompass both the Vedas and tantra.

There are many interpretations of the word Sri Vidya which can mean Great knowledge (*mahavidya*), knowledge of sacrifice (*yajnavidya*), and the knowledge of Self (*Atmavidya*). This tantra, which is considered one of the most precious, is a synthesis of the Vedic and non-vedic practices. This may also be called the knowledge of Divine Mother, Sri Mata (Tripura-sundary) and even Brahman.

Sri Vidya worship is also undertaken to acquire supernatural and healing powers or siddhis and the practice incorporates mantra, yantra, astrology, numerology, meditation, rituals and offerings.

There are three kinds or kramas of Sri vidya: kalikrama (kundalinikrama, kadividya) in which the sattvaguna is predominant, Sundarikrama (Hamsakrama, Hadi vidya) in which 'rajas' is dominant and Tarakrama (Samavarodhini krama, Sadi Vidya) in which 'tamas' is supreme. There are also three main sects called Hayagriva, Anandabhairava and Dakshinamurti who are the follwers of Sri Vidya.

There are eight major siddhis which can be acquired through Sri Vidya. They are *Paushtika karma* (health and healing), *shanti karma* (peace and happiness), *marana* (hurting and killing), *vashikarana* (subjugating and dominating), *mohana* (for confusion and delusion), *unchhatana* (frustrating and disrupting), *vidveshana* (creating hatred), and *stambhana* (making a person immobile). The great spiritul masters, as we have mentioned earlier, look down upon the cheap display of siddhis especially when they lead to destruction. They emphasise that the ultimate goal of the student is to merge with the Divine.

We shall not consider the details regarding the prerequisites to be fulfiled by the student and other necessary precautions that need to be taken. The practice say, of healing consists of a number of steps. We shall only consider the following steps which are of interest from the standpoint of Om.

The practitioners use peculiar mantras for imbuing a (numerical) yantra with the power of the deity - the ritual called pranapratishtha which we have already mentioned. One such mantra is:

Om am hrim yam ram lam vam sham *sh*am sam ham hamsah soham mama asmin yantre mama ishta devah ihaivagatya sukham chiram tishthatu svaha. Om Om Om pratishtha.

Note the abundance of the bijas and adibija (Om).

Another yantra used at a higher step consists of 25 small squares within a square. The yantra has tridents or trishulas (symbolizing Shiva) along its boundary.

In the squarish slots, one finds 'namah Shivaya' written in rows as well as columns. This is a part of a revered mantra.

Om namah Shivaya
(Om, hail to Shiva).

'Namah Shivaya' is called panchakshara (five - lettered) and is said to be effective only when the inscriptions are in the Devanagari script because the tantriks believe that the script is a yantra itself ('Deva' means god).

Sri yantra or Sri chakra is a yantra associated with Sri Vidya. There appear to be many types of Sri yantra,

Sri Yantra

but the most revered yantra is shown here:

The mulamantra of Sri Vidya is based on "ka e ee la hreem, hreem ha sa ka ha la sa ka la hreem". Since the bijas are 15 in number. Sri Vidya is also called *panchadashi vidya.*

We have mentioned the process of energising an idol or yantra, called prana pratishtha. There are rules of the location of the yantra connected with the type of prana pratishtha. In case of *achara* ('stationary') pranapratishtha, the yantra has to be kept at one place. If the prana pratishtha is *chara* ('mobile'), the yantra can be transferred to another place subject to certain conditions using specific rituals. If the yantra is meant for *dharana* ('wearing'), it has to be removed at the time of a puja. After the completion of the puja it can be worn again after chanting a specific mantra.

Twelve

YOGA

"The yogi who wears but a *godedi* (shawl made of waste cloth pieces), who walks the path that is beyond merit and demerit, whose mind is joined in perfect yoga with its goal, he reveals (in God-consciousness) and lives thereafter as a child or as a madman ...."

—Shankara in *Bhaja Govindam* (22)

To the lay person, 'yoga' means Patanjali's raja yoga or hatha yoga in which the yogi assumes complicated postures. The word, however, has a much wider connotation. Etymologically, it means union : the union between the individual soul and the Universal Soul. It indicates a path of liberation from the cycle of birth and death or realisation of the Ultimate Reality.

Since Om is Brahman as well as a sacred mantra, importance of pranava is paramount in most systems of yoga. In what follows we can only briefly describe the different systems of yoga.

1. *Jnana yoga* — This is the path of realising that the self (Atman) is not different from Brahman, the Ultimate Reality. In this connection we recall our comments on Vedanta especially the monistic philosophy of advaita.

2. *Sankhya yoga* — This is akin to jnana yoga but appeals to those who accept the dualistic philosophy. This path asks you to realize that the

body is different from the soul: the former is destructible and feels the pairs of opposites; pain and pleasure, love and hate. The latter is eternal and immortal. When you are above the feelings of I and mine, you become a Brahmajnani and merge into Brahman which is not different from Om. Chapter 2 of the *Bhagvad Gita* discusses this yoga.

3. *Karma yoga* — This path described in chapter 3 of the *Bhagvad Gita*, exhorts you to perform your duties without attachment and without expecting any fruits of action. This yoga is suitable for householders.

4. *Japa yoga* — This yoga consists of repeating a mantra. The most sacred mantra is, of course, Om which symbolises Brahman, but other mantras such as the Gayatri are also considered efficacious. These are Vedic mantras. The mantras from Puranas in which other gods Rama, Krishna, Vishnu, Hanumana etc., are worshipped are also recommended along with idol worship.

However, for saints like Swami Ramadasa of 17th century, even a simple mantra such as "Hare Rama" is equally good: one need not be a scholar of the Vedas to use the japa yoga.

Japas are classified on the basis of other criteria too. Nityajapa is to be performed daily. Naimittika japa is to be performed on specific occasions. Prayashchitta japa indicates the japa to wash off sins. The japa may be chanted loudly or murmured or said only in the mind. In Akhanda japa the worshipper undertakes chanting without interruption (*khanda*). We have already mentioned the ajapa japa which is natural and in tune with breathing — Soham, which also contains Om or AUM.

5. *Bhakti yoga* — This is the path of worship which is elaborated in chapter 12 of the *Bhagvad Gita* which deals with two forms of worship; that of the manifest deity (*saguna Brahman*) and the unmanifest one, Om or Brahman (*nirguna Brahman*).

   Scriptures prescribe many types of bhakti such as hearing God's glories (*shravana*), remembering God (*smarana*), praying (*vandana*), describing God's glories (*kirtana*) etc. Om plays an important role in most of these types as a repeated symbol of Brahman.

6. *Mantra Yoga* — This is sometimes identified with japa yoga mentioned above. However, some scholars prescribe a sixteen-step mantra yoga which includes *bhakti, shuddhi* (purification), *asana* (seat or posture), *panchanga savana* (reading of five scriptures), *achara, havana* (offering), mudra etc., culminating in samadhi. Om is used at several stages.

7. *Patanjali yoga* — This was briefly discussed under darshana in chapter 2. This is also called ashtanga ('eight limbs') yoga or raja ('royal') yoga. This yoga based on Patanjali's Yoga Sutras (2nd century CE) consists of eight stages.

   I   Self-control (*yama*). The five yamas are non-violence (*ahimsa*), truthfulness (*satya*), non-stealing (*asteya*), celibacy (*bhrahmacharya*) and non-possessiveness (*aparigraha*).

II   Observance of rules (*niyama*).

      There are five niyamas viz., internal and external purity (*shaucha*), contentment (*santosha*), austerity and perseverence (*tapas*), study of scriptures (*svadhyaya*) and dedication to God of actions and will (*Ishvara pranidhana*).

III   Posture (*asana*) — It is necessary to choose the correct posture suited to one's constitution. Many asanas are described in scriptures.

IV   Control of breath or vital force (*pranayama*). There are ten different pranas of which inhaling (also called prana) and exhaling (apana) were mentioned in connection with the Om-encompassing Soham.

V   Withdrawal of mind from sense objects (*pratyahara*).

VI   Concentration (*dharana*) — This involves concentration on a suitable object to steady your mind.

VII   Meditation (*dhyana*) — In this, the mind becomes one-pointed.

VIII *Samadhi* — This is the last stage which gives the sadhaka a trance-like state. In the first phase, samadhi is *sabija* or 'with seed' in which the yogi maintains his individuality. The final phase is the *nirbija* (seedless) samadhi in which the practitioner's individuality is lost and she enters the true superconscious state. While Patanjali's text contains extremely laconic sutras, they have been interpreted by many scholars. In the first chapter Samadhipadah sutras 27-31 extol the virtues of Om:

Pranava or Om is another name for Ishvara or God which appears in innumerable forms. Om emanates perpetually from the primary abode of Ishvara (Purusha) and Prakriti. Om is the power that controls the whole universe. In samadhi, yogis hear precisely this sound in their supreconscious state. As we have already mentioned Om is A-U-M. A for Agni-Vishnu, U for Hiranyagarbha, Shiva or Brilliance and M for the attainment of God (Ishvara — Prakriti duo). This is the reason why Om should be recited by the sadhaka.

There are many obstacles a yogi faces, but the japa of Om removes these hurdles and brings the yogi closer to God. When the yogi meditates on different qualities of God, he himself acquires those qualities.

The japa of Om gradually expands your inner vision and all physical and mental obstacles are removed.

Patanjali also mentions the nature of different obstacles which can be countered by the yogi through Om and other practices. These impediments are :

1. *Vyadhi* — disease, inactivity of senses, delusions etc.
2. *Styana* — lack of enthusiasm, inability to cope with the sadhana.
3. *Samshaya* — Doubt about one's own abilities.
4. *Pramada* — Lack of concentration and discontinuation of sadhana.
5. *Alasya* — Laziness.
6. *Avirati* — Absence of detachment to worldly objects, attraction to sex and passion.
7. *Bhrantidarshana* — Delusion to the effect that yoga is not efficacious.
8. *Alabdhabhumitattva* — Inability to attain one-pointedness.

9. *Anavasthittva* - Withdrawal from the higher state to lower state.

10. Unhappiness, which can be spiritual, mental or somatic; passion, anger, jealousy, worry, fear are responsible for such a state.

11. Despondency on account of non-attainment of goal.

12. Panic or physical shaking.

13. Inability to maintain steady breathing, forcible inhaling or forcible excessive exhaling.

8. *Dhyana Yoga* — This path uses the seventh stage 'dhyana' of the Patanjali yoga. Meditation is the most important route to know Ishvara. In *sthula dhyana* you concentrate on an object which you see with your eyes or can visualise in the mind. You can meditate on different gods; Rama, Shiva, Krishna, Ganesha etc., whose idols are either before you or in your mind. There are other types of dhyana called *sukshma* ('minute') dhyana or *jyotidhyana* (*jyoti* for 'flame'). The latter is used by tantriks.

9. *Tantra Yoga* — A generic term used for a yoga which incorporates tantric methods.

10. *Kundalini Yoga* — A type of tantra yoga in which the sadhaka awakens the kundalini, and raises her to the sahasrara. When the Mother Kundalini reaches Shiva's abode, the yogi experiences indescribable ecstacy and merges with the Divine Mother. This yoga is also called 'bhuta shuddhi'. The yogi has to bring back the kundalini to her original place viz., muladhara. In this connection it is necessary to mention that the yogi uses

'hunkara' to rouse Devi Kundalini at a certain stage. 'Hum', it must be remembered, is an important bija closely related to and emanating from 'Om'. You can read a detailed discussion of the kundalini arousal in John Woodroffe's book, *The Serpent Power.*

11. *Hatha Yoga* — 'Hatha' means force. This yoga seeks liberation through purification of body and consciousness. The yoga developed by Natha yogis between ninth and eleventh centuries uses first four stages of the Patanjali yoga. It also incorporates such practices as *dhauti* which cleanses the stomach, *neti* which cleans the nose with threads and *kapala bhati* which scavenges the nasal passage and sinuses.

Hatha Yoga lays considerable stress on the power of sperm (bindu). With proper exercises, the yogis try to raise the bindu to the sahsrara which incidentally aids the kundalini to ascend. When the kundalini reaches the sahasrara, there is a shower of amrita or elixir. Using what is called the khechari mudra, the yogi drinks the nectar, without allowing it to pass downwards.

12. *Kriya Yoga* — The yoga consists of the three of the niyamas prescribed in the raja yoga, austerity (tapas), study of scriptures (svadhyaya) and surrender to god (Ishvara pranidhana). Svadhyaya involves not only reading the Vedas, Upanishads and other shastras but also doing good deeds and the japa of Om and Gayatri. Similarly Ishvara pranidhana includes worship which in turn regards meditation and the japa of Om as the most precious.

13. *Laya Yoga* — This is the yoga of dissolution which is mentioned in Shankara's *Yoga Taravali*. You will recall that the anahata is called the chakra of unstruck sound. This is associated with the primordial syllable Om. The yogi trains himself to hear this sound. The posture called *siddhasana* is believed to be the suitable asana. With vaishnavi mudra, the yogi listens to this sound through the right ear, shutting off the external sound.

    Gradually, the yogi or 'masters' pranava or Aum. With perseverance the yogi reaches the turiya state or the state of superconsciousness. He has gradually dissolved into the world-soul.

14. *Suratashabda Yoga* — This yoga, too, lays emphasis on the 'inner sound'. It believes that we have two indentities, the manifest and concealed. Through the inner sound we can reach the hidden self. This activates the various chakras that have hidden powers. With prolonged practice the yogi merges into the Supreme Being.

15. *Taraka Yoga* — The yoga asks you to meditate on the centre between the eyebrows. With sufficient practice you will begin to see the hidden brilliance which is the manifestation of the sun and the moon inside the head (mind). You will ultimately encounter the Supreme Being that is pure consciousness, truth and bliss. The yoga is explained in the *Taraka Upanishad*.

16. *Sahaja Yoga* — This yoga has become popular in recent times and is aimed at activating the kundalini. It is suitable for householders. 'Sahaja' means easy. You have to devote some time to

dhyana every day. We have already mentioned the importance of Om in dhyana.

17. *Adhyatma Yoga* in *Yogavasishtha* — In literature on spiritualism (*adhyatma*) *Yogavasishtha Maharamayanali* has great importance. It contains a dialogue between Rama and the guru Vasishtha in which knowledge, yoga and other methods of liberation are discussed. This will be considered in chapter 13.

18. *Yoga in Shrimadbhagvat* — *Shrimadbhagvat* is an important Puranic text. It contains a yoga which incorporates eight limbs of the raja yoga, but it lays more stress on bhakti or worship. The yoga, *inter alia,* specifies a method of purifying prana through inhaling, stoppage of breath and exhaling. After this, the pranava of three matras (moras) AUM must be recited in the mind.

Yoga in *The Bhagavad Gita*

Every chapter of this scripture is called a yoga:

1. Arjunavishada yoga — The despondency of Arjuna.
2. Sankhya yoga — The yoga of knowledge
3. Karma yoga — The yoga of action
4. Jnanakarmasanyas yoga — The yoga of renunciation of action in knowledge.
5. Sanyasa yoga — The yoga of renunciation
6. Dhyana yoga — The yoga of meditation
7. Jnanavijnana yoga — The yoga of knowledge and realisation.
8. Aksharabrahma yoga — The yoga of the imperishable Brahman.
9. Rajavidyarajaguhya yoga — The yoga of sovereign science and sovereign secret.

10. Vibhuti yoga — The yoga of divine manifestation.
11. Vishvarupadarshana yoga — The yoga of the vision of the cosmic form.
12. Bhakti yoga — The yoga of devotion.
13. Kshetrakshetrajnavibhaga yoga — The yoga of the discrimination of the kshetra and kshetrajna.
14. Gunatrayavibhaga yoga — The yoga of the division of the three gunas.
15. Purushottama yoga — The yoga of the Supreme Self.
16. Daivasurasampadvibhaga yoga — The yoga of division between the divine and the demoniacal.
17. Shraddhatrayavibhaga yoga — The yoga of the three fold shraddha.
18. Mokshasanyasa yoga — The yoga of liberation by renunciation.

Many of these yogas refer to Om or its equivalent Brahman or Atman.

It is impossible even to discuss briefly all these 'yogas', but in the chapter on the Bhagvad Gita we have highlighted those yogas in which Om or pranava has a prominent place.

Yoga in Buddhism

The Buddhist yogis follow a six-stage yoga. These limbs are akin to the latter six steps of the raja yoga. They are (1.) pratyahara (2.) dhyana (3.) pranayana (4.) dharana (5.) anusmriti and (6.) samadhi.

The pranayama does not consist of puraka-rechaka-kumbhaka but a five-fold ritual. The 'prana complex' believed to be present at the tip of the nose is meditated upon as if there were five gems or five effulgent beams of light. The practice of anusmriti makes the yogi see unity in diversity. Meditation on this One leads to samadhi. The Tibetan lamas spin a wheel with one hand and recite the mantra.

Om mani padme hum

Scholars believe that this *mani padme yoga* helps the kundalini shakti break the manipura chakra or lotus (padma) and helps the lama in reaching the superconscious state.

According to Shankaracharya (108) Shri Yogeshvaranandatirtha of Jagannathapuri, it was a brahmin Padmasambhava who introduced Vajrayana or mantrayana school of Buddhism in Tibet. According to him in mantrayana Vajravarahi and Tara enjoy the status of deities. Omkara in Vedic religion as well as in Buddhism is called Tara, its feminine counterpart being called Tar*aa*.

The worshippers of the manipadma also recite the mantra:

Hum manipadme hum

which is believed by scholars as corruption of

Om manipadme Om

In Jainism Paramatman is called Panchaparameshthi. Its main mantra is : Namo Arihanta*n*am ˇNamo siddha*n*am ˇNamo loe sabbasahu*n*am

(Pronounce *n* as n in 'and')

From this mahamantra, 'arihanasiddha' 'asi-a-u-sa', 'arihanta, 'siddha', and Om have been derived as mantras upto five syllables.

We have already mentioned that samadhi is a trance-like state. It is said of Swami Ramakrishna that he went into samadhi all of a sudden without any indication of the prior stages and remained in the hypnotic state for an indefinite period. It is believed that Om provided on 'antidote' to his trance. Paradoxical though it may sound a prolonged trance without prior notice was an embarrassment to his disciples. Fortunately, the very pranava which helped one to attain samadhi also could extricate one entangled in spiritual hypnotism. It may seem that a homeopathic principle was at work in the process.

Thirteen

YOGA VASISHTHA

"Those who renounce work and rely on fate (*bhagya*) are their own enemies."

—*Yoga Vasishtha* (2-7-3)

The *Bhagvad Gita* records Krishna's consolation of and advice given to Arjuna who was despondent before the war against his close relatives, began. It is not known widely that Rama who is believed to be Vishnu's incarnation received similar counselling by Rishi Vasishtha.

Rama is the hero of the epic the *Ramayana* and the eldest son of Dasharatha a king of the solar race which reigned at Ayodhya. When he was about to enter adulthood, Rama went on a long pilgrimage. When he returned to Ayodhya, he appeared to be depressed and disgusted with the earthly life. Vasishtha, who is called Brahma's 'mind-son', consoled Rama and imparted to him the knowledge which he himself had received from Brahma. The sage's sermon is believed to have had a salutary effect on Rama, who not only regained peace of mind, but also realised Brahman.

The *Yoga Vasishtha* contains nearly 30,000 verses and discusses such topics as Atman, Brahman, Realization (moksha), jnana, yoga, shanti and Om. A brief discussion of this text will enable you to recapitulate the concepts which we have already discussed. When viewed through the lense of the *Yoga Vasishtha* The sermon delivered to Rama has a peculiar kind of freshness and clarity. Vasishtha subscribes to what may be called extreme advaitism. Like Dattatreya, author of the *Avadhuta Gita*, Vasishtha accepts non-dualism as a fact and the question of 'liberation' does not arise. If we feel that bonds or fetters exist, it is only because of our illusion. Hence we can only talk of dispelling illusion (maya) that we are different from Brahman. We may thus speak of realisation and not of liberation.

Atman and Brahman

According to Vasishtha, there is only one Reality, Atman or Brahman which is eternal, formless, indescribable, omnipotent, quiescent and omnipresent.

The appearance of the universe (*jagat*) is only an illusion, only a vibration of Brahman. Since the universe does not exist in reality, it is foolish to say that Brahman 'created' it.

The individual jiva is nothing but Brahman. What we call action (karma) is not different from the body which is identical with the chitta. The chitta is not different from the ego and jiva. The jiva is Ishvara, Atman and Parama Shiva. The mind is not different from Brahman. What we call Prakriti (nature) is none other than Brahman.

It is for those who are devoid of true knowledge that we speak of such differences as doer (karta), action (karma), earth, flora and fauna, birth, death etc. Actually all those are the ever-peaceful Brahman. The delusion of division is created by avidya (nescience) or maya.

I am Brahman, you are Brahman, every form is Brahman, the whole universe is Brahman. In reality there does not exist either the seer or what he sees. There is neither the waking state, nor sleep, nor sushupti (dreamless sleep), nor even turiya. Everything is Brahman in peace.

However, Vasishtha adds that the knowledge of advaita should be imparted only to those who are fit to receive it — as Rama, according to the sage, was. You will be wasting your time if you try to preach this sermon to an idiot, a fool, and a person who runs after the sense objects.

We have used the word shanti in chapter 7. This word connotes more than just peace. In this text it can mean quietude, indifference, non-resistance, inactivity and so on depending on the context. As we shall see, according to Vasishtha, shanti plays a vital role in the knowledge of Brahman and moksha.

The Knowledge of Atman or Atmajnana

According to Vasishtha avidya is the cause of misery. Misery arises from desire. It is only when desire vanishes and shanti prevails, that unhappiness can disappear. What you need is the peaceful mind or chitta. You have to withdraw your senses from the sense-objects and concentrate on Reality which is Atman or Brahman.

Nirvana in which Supreme Bliss prevails can be attained only through *atmajnana.* The knowledge of Self is our ultimate goal which leads to shanti and realisation.

The prerequisites of atmajnana are shanti, contentment, and association with sadhus. A person is called shantatma who is not affected by sound, touch, smell, and who does not yield to anger or jealousy.

Supreme bliss is that which lies in seeing Atman and Brahman in yourself as well as in objects.

People often speak of fate (bhagya) as the cause of their happiness and misery. We have to understand that our own actions or *purushartha* determine our future. It is important to realise that instead of running away from your work you should follow purushartha according to scriptures.

Bondage and Realisation (moksha)

What we call bondage (*bandhana*) and moksha are mere delusions arising from avidya. When we do not see non-duality we feel illusory fetters and search for moksha. In reality we are always free, not different from Atman or Brahman.

People often talk of two types of mokshas, (1) *jivanmukti* in which a person is 'liberated' during his or her lifetime, (2) *videhamukti* when she is free after death and is not reborn. But if you look inside, you will find that the concept of liberation is wrong. You have always been free — it is your avidya which makes you feel that you are a prisoner.

If you engage yourself in your work in a disinterested manner and have no attachment you will realise that there is only shanti - bondage is an illusion.

It is necessary to realise that what we call karma (action, work) is nothing but the vibration of our mind. It is the *desire* which makes you feel that you are bonded when you perform work. Do your work without any expectations of fruits.

It is not necessary for you to renounce work: renounce desire. Realise that desire is not a part of your real self which is Atman.

Remember, the only way to moksha is atmajnana. Pilgrimage, renunciation, austerity, charity, yajna etc., may lead you to heaven, but it is only atmajnana which gives you moksha.

Seven Steps to Moksha

Vasishtha mentions seven prerequisites for moksha which according to him is the knowledge (jnana) of Truth.

The first requirement is called shubhechha (*shubha* for auspicious *ichha* for wish). A person has shubhechha when he has a desire to be detached and acquire jnana through scriptures and sages. When, through detachment and practice, he desires to follow scripturally approved conduct, his wish is called *vicharana*. When he develops indifference towards sense-objects, his mind has become 'less gross', a state called *tanumanasa*. The next stage is *sattvapatti* in which the person is absorbed in Atman. This leads to his withdrawal from the external world and he is stable in the brilliance of Atman. He has reached the stage of *asmasakti*. In the next stage he gains the knowledge that all things, internal as well as external, are illusory. This is the stage of *padarthabhavana*. When dualism has disappeared and the person is one with Atman he has reached the stage called *turiya*. The first three stages constitute wakefulness, the fourth stage is comparable with the sleep with dreams. A person who has reached this stage is *tattvajnani*. The fifth and sixth states constitute what Vashistha calls jivanamukti. According to him, a person who goes beyond turiya has become videhamukta. This stage is also called mukti, Brahman or nirvana.

Pranava, Yoga and Jnana

According to Vasishtha there are two methods to reach the state of chitta (mind) shanti. One is yoga and the other is jnana. While he gives supreme importance to jnana, he also mentions yoga as a means to attain moksha.

He calls a person jnani whose passions and desires have disappeared, whose work and moral actions are without attachment, and who has realised that Atman and Brahman are the Ultimate Reality. It is necessary to persevere when one wants to obtain this wisdom. The jnana that you are the Truth or Brahman is also called *tattva*.

Vasishtha defines yoga as a method to 'cross' samsara or transcend the mundane existence. This involves effecting the state of shanti of the mind. In a broad sense, atmajnana is also a yoga, but he reserves the word yoga for the practice in which prana is brought under control to attain shanti.

Yoga proper can be practiced in three ways as follows:

(1) Make your mind stable and peaceful. Renounce attachment. Sitting comfortably, recite the mantra Om, Om, Om... till your mind gains shanti. Dissolve the body, senses, mind and buddhi in those tattvas from where they have arisen. Dissolve yourself in the great expanse of the (apparent) universe. You will find that there is no jagat or the world and your avidya and maya will disappear. You will merge with the Ultimate Reality, Brahman.

(2) In this yogic method you control (pacify) your prana and obtain shanti. Vasishtha mentions puraka(inhaling), rechaka (exhaling) and kumbhaka (retaining the breath). Using these, you

have to practise pranayama or the control of breath. Vasishtha also believes that there is external (*bhya*) pranayama with external counterparts of inner puraka, rechaka and kumbhaka. The idea is to control both pranas inside and outside your body and bring about shanti which makes you reach *kevala pada* which is the realisation of your freedom. This process of controlling prana is also called *nirodha*. This involves stoppage of the vibrations of prana.

One of the ingredients of this sadhana is recitation of Omkara. When Om is chanted, you understand the tattva of sound which helps you reach the sushupta stage. This aids in arresting the vibrations of prana. The sage mentions several ancillary methods to quieten prana and attain shanti which is nothing but moksha.

(3) The third yogic method is to use your will power to quieten your mind and reach shanti. Reading of scriptures, association with saintly people, renunciation of desire and control of prana are used as ancillary aids.

Kundalini Yoga

Vasishtha also explains how siddhis can be acquired. He asserts that the shakti is in the form of a coil (*kundali*) hence the name kundalini. According to him it is the seed of five senses of knowledge. He also says that the kundalini is stationed in a nadi called *antraveshtanika* ("that which is surrounded inside"). The nadi has the form resembling the lower part of the instrument veena and also looks like a vortex in a sea. He also likens it with the half part of the letter Om. He explains that the kundalini is aroused for siddhis as well as realisation.

Agni-Soma Vichara Yoga

The sage tells us that in the heart (anahata chakra) are stationed the sun and the moon. After mentioning that the kundalini serpent when aroused ascends via the sushumna nadi, he describes its status when it rests in the "heart-lotus". He calls her kundalini Lakshmi. When in the heart, she is responsible for the production of the sound Om or pranava. She also emits prana and apana.

Their union gives rise to churning, leading to the production of Agni which appears in akasha (ether). The inside of the heart is then illuminated. Prana represents the sun and apana the moon, and they are called Agni-Soma. Their union leads the yogi to realise that he is none other than Atman or Brahman, the ultimate One.

The importance of shanti is made clear when Rama after hearing Vasishtha, regains his confidence and says, "I am free from anger and jealousy I feel surrounded by supreme shanti. All my doubts have disappeared. I see only Brahman."

Fourteen

YOGA, GODS AND PRANAVA

"The word Om is like the sky, it is not the discernment of the essence of high and low. How can there be enunciation of the point of the word (Om) which nullifies the manifestation of the Unmanifest?"

—Dattatreya in *Avadhuta Gita* (5-1)

In chapters 2 through 5 we considered a few major Upanishads. In this chapter we shall briefly discuss three groups of Upnanishads which though not considered major Upanishads, are extremely important for us.

In the first group are Upanishads which discuss the yogic methods of emancipation. There are about eleven of them, but we shall discuss only (1) Brahmavidya ('knowledge of Brahman') (2) Nadabindu ('sound point') (3) Amritabindu ('elixir point') (4) Dhyanabindu ('meditation point') (4) Yogatattva ('essence of yoga').

The second group consists of Upanishads in which individual deities are treated as Brahman. We shall consider (1) Shiva Upanishads viz., (a) Atharvashiras ("the main point of the Atharvaveda") (b) Atharvashikha ("tip of the Atharva") (c) Kalignirudra (2) Vishnu Upanishads, viz. (a) Narayana (b) Nrisimha (man-lion) (c) Rama. In the third group we shall discuss an extremely important Upanishad viz., Pranava (Pranou) relating to Om.

Yoga Upanishads

Brahmavidya

This small Yoga Upanishad has a peculiar approach to Om.

Verse 3 declares that Om is Brahman. It describes in verses 4-7 what is called the body of the sound Om. The first three matras are identified as follows:

Sound	Veda	Fire	Worlds	Gods
a	Rig	Garhapatya	Earth	Brahma
u	Yajus	Dakshina	Sky	Vishnu
m	Sama	Ahavaniya	Heaven	Shiva

It, then mentions that Om is located in the brain-conch (*shankha*); 'a' shines as the sun, 'u' as the moon and 'm' as fire. The half-matra rises like a pointed flame (*shikha*).

Verses 11-12 speak of the terminus (*kala*) of the sound. Its meaning is not very clear but Deussen interprets it as follows : when the end(kala) is near, Om breaks through the sun in the brain as well as 7200 arteries, penetrates the head through Brahmarandhram and reaches a point where it becomes all creative and all penetrating.

The last verse relates to the vanishing of sound or laya. The sound Om fades away gradually like that of the gong which is struck. The peace (shanti) in which it dies is Brahman, for Om (*dhruva*) itself is Brahman and helps towards immortality.

Nadabindu

This has been translated by Deussen as "the secret meaning of the nasal-point". 'Bindu' here refers to the anusvara which denotes the third matra of Om as also the vibration of the half-matra.

According to this Upanishad, liberation can be attained by yogis only through meditation on Om along with renunciation of all sense perception.

It also says that each of the four moras has three-fold aspect from which three objects (or matras) of meditation (12 objects in all) arise.

	Object	Characteristics
1.	Ghoshini	Rich in sound
2.	Vidyunmali	Wreathed in lightning
3.	Patangi	Flight enjoyer
4.	Vayuvegini	Swift
5.	Namadheya	Namable
6.	Aindri	Sacred to Indra
7.	Vaishnavi	Vishnu
8.	Shankari	Shiva
9.	Mahati	Great
10.	Dhruva	Firm
11.	Mauni	Silent
12.	Brahmi	Brahmic

Meditation on each object at the time of death gives the yogi one reward. For instance, if he meditates on Ghoshini, he is born as king in the next life. When the twelfth object is meditated upon, the yogi is liberated and he reaches the 'eternal light of Brahman'. The highest reward of the yoga is becoming Brahman which is the same as going 'into the highest bliss'.

Amrita-bindu or Amrita-nada

This Upanishad condemns all bookish learning. It also considers the sound of Om as only the means to the end viz., liberation. It is only the soundless 'm' (*asvaramakara*) which is also symbolised by the anusvara (bindu) point that is to be meditated upon.

Dhyanabindu

This contains the doctrine of point (bindu). The yogi is asked to meditate on the bindu of Om. It also explains how Om should be pronounced. It contends that it is reverberation of the tip of Om (the half-matra) which contains the true knowledge. It asks the yogi to identify with the arrow and treat Om as bow and Brahman as the target. It asks him to look upon the Om-sound as the upper stick and himself as the friction-wood. The yogi should use the half matra as a rope and draw up the heart-lotus to the place between the brows where Atman or Brahman rests.

Yogatattva

In this Upanishad, Om is depicted as all-comprehensive, encompassing the three worlds, the three Vedas and the three gunas. The yogi who meditates at the end of the tri-syllable i.e., the half-matra of Aum, pervades through all this and reaches the highest point.

According to this Upanishad the manas is situated in the heart-lotus. With the a-sound of Aum, it becomes luminous, with u-sound it opens up, with 'm' it resounds. The half-matra is motionless and shines in the soul of the yogi imbuing him with the highest spirit of yoga.

Shiva Upanishads

The Shiva Upanishads look upon Shiva as Atman.

Atharvashiras "The main point of the Atharvaveda."

This Upanishad regards Rudra (Ishana, Bhagvan, Maheshvara) as the past, present and the future, and

all-embracing having the symbol of Om-sound. Rudra
(the word Shiva is not mentioned in the text) is called
the 'greatest swallower'. His head is to the North and is
identified with Om. He is also the holy call (pranava)
because he is all-pervading. He is called the sound Om
because being uttered, he makes the breaths ascend.

The first matra 'a' of Aum has Brahma as the deity
and its colour is red. He who meditates on it
continuously, reaches the abode of Brahman. The
second matra 'u' has Vishnu as devata and its colour is
black. Meditating on it takes one to Vishnu. The third
matra is brown and its deity is Ishana. He who meditates
on it goes to Ishana. But the last half-matra has all these
gods and one who meditates on it reaches the house
of Bliss.

Atharvashikha

This Upanishad is closely related to the previous one.
It interprets the matras as follows:

Matra	World	Veda	Main God	Colour
a	Earth	Rig	Brahma	Red
u	Sky	Yajur	Vishnu	Black
m	Heaven	Sama	Rudra	White
1/2 matra		Atharva	Ekarishi	All coloured
(reverbe-ration)			(Purusha. Ishana)	

The Upanishad mentions that the Om-sound has four
quarters, the fourth quarter being a half matra. It is
pronounced audibly in three ways; Om (short), Omm
(long), Ommm (extra long). The fourth way is the calm-
self (shantatman). This should come suddenly when Om
is chanted in an extra-long manner. This is like

revelation when the buzzing of 'm' has disappeared and supreme silence follows. It is the supreme way that is the true Om-sound or Omkara. The last 1/2 matra is also identified with the Atharvaveda, the fire of universal destruction, Maruts and the Viraj the wisest. This matra is self-effulgent.

Om is also called Pranava because it makes all the Pranas bow down to itself.

Kalignirudra

This Upanishad describes the significance of *tripundram*, a mark from ashes consisting of three streaks which those belonging to a shaiva sect make on the forehead, cranium, shoulder and the breast with ancillary mantras.

According to the Upanishad the first line is Garhapatya (fire), the a-sound of Om, the rajas guna, the terrestrial world, external Atman, the power of action, the Rigveda, and the morning pressing of Soma. Its deity is Maheshvara. The second line is the Dakshina fire, u-sound of Aum, atmosphere, the rajas guna, the inner Atman, will-power, the Yajus and the midday pressing of Soma. Its deity is Sadashiva. The third line is the Adhvaniya fire, m-sound of pranava, the tamas guna, the highest Atman, power of perception, The Samaveda and the evening pressing. Its divinity is Shiva.

It is interesting to note that all gods named are none other than Rudra. The Upanishad also says that the person who performs the ritual relating to tripundram gives up the body and merges with Shiva.

Vishnu Upanishads

In these Upanishads Vishnu or Narayana is praised and equated with Atman or Brahman. In the *Maha Upanishad*,

Narayana is depicted as the first existence prior to the appearance of Brahma, Ishana (Shiva) and the world.

Narayana

This text exhorts you to utter the octo-syllabic metrical line, "Om namo Narayana". If you study this line, you will reach the full span of life, without any difficulties, be happy and have offsprings and prosperity.

You will have the inner bliss, and Narayana, Brahman, Purusha will enter you fusing a, u, m into Aum and becoming one with pranava.

The yogi who sees this greatness and a person who worships *Om namo Narayana* reaches Vaikuntha where Vishnu resides.

Nrisimha-Purva-Tapaniya and Nrisimha-Uttara-Tapaniya Upanishamds

These Upanishads are in praise of Nrisimha who is an avataar of Vishnu and is half man and half lion.

The Purva Upanishad mentions that when Prajapati practised penance he saw the Mantraraja (royal formula) relating to Nrisimha. The 'formula' deals with four world-regions which Prajapati created using Mantraraja.

According to this text all Vedas have Om-sound in the beginning. Those who know that Om is the limb of this formula, conquer the world. The four lines of the formula are also identified, *inter alia*, with a, u, m and the half-matra of Aum which is the 'Soma world'. The last half matra is also the Om itself.

Pranava is the first *anga* (part) of Mantraraja. Om is the whole world, the past, the present and the future. It is also Brahman and Atman.

In this Upanishad Prajapati explains the details of the 'Great Circle' or *Sudarshanam* which is the discus of Vishnu. Yogis use this diagram in their sadhana. At the centre of this circle is the delivering sign *tarakam* which means Nrisimha as well as Om. The gist of the Uttara Upanishad is the following formula :

Atman = Om = Brahman = Narasimha

Like the Mandukya Upanishad, this text divides Atman into four states:

(1) the waking and the gross world of waking
(2) the dream and the subtle dream-world.
(3) the deep sleep or the seed world
(4) The Turiya or the fourth state of Witness in which there is a union between the subject and the object. This Upanishad, however, goes further: it analyses Turiya into:

(1) Atman the fourth state of Witness is akin to *ota* ('woven into' the world) as the world is to the rays of 'time-fire'.

(2) Atman who is *anujnatri* (affirmer) of the universe since it gives it its own self and makes it visible as the sun influences the darkness.

(3) Atman who is *anujna* (affirmation) : by its very nature, it is pure thought similar to the fire that has consumed the fuel.

(4) Atman who is *avikalpa* (indifference) since it cannot be expressed in words and thoughts.

In the same way, Om that is none other than Turiya has corresponding aspects : In-woven, Assenter, Assent and Indifference.

The Upanishad propounds a conception in which Turiya projects, by means of Om, into the external object. It is not possible to wholly describe what the text says about Om. The following statements should capture the essence:

1. The Atman, the highest Brahman shines as Turiya at the tip of the Om-sound.
2. Each of A, U, M of pranava is Atman, Brahman and Nrisimha.
3. A-U-M = Atman-lion-Atman
    = Atman-consent-Brahman
    = Brahman-consent-Atman
4. Om (Atman, Brahman,) is the Reality. It is soundless (fourth matra), touchless, formless, odourless, without the manas, buddhi, chitta, without prana, without sense-organs, without gunas, without objects and marks and is unborn. What's more, it is without maya.

Rama Purva - Tapaniya and Rama-Uttara-Tapaniya Upanishads

These are in some ways similar to the Nrisimha Upanishad, but another avatara, Rama, of Vishnu replaces Narasimha. It extols Om and analyses the matras of Om. The Uttara Upanishad distinguishes six elements; a, u, m, half-matra, bindu and nada and asserts that those who know Om will attain to *Avimuktam* (Shiva) and liberation.

At one place 'a' is identified with Lakshmana (Rama's half brother), 'u' with Shatrughna (Rama's half-brother) and 'm' with Bharata (another half-brother). The half matra is identified with Rama. The entire Om is identified with Sita, (Rama's wife) as *Mulaprakriti*.

The Purva Upanishad describes a yantra or diagram. At the centre of the yantra is inscribed.

Om *Ram* Om

Ram is a monosyllable which unlike 'Rama' is nasalised.

Pranava (Pranou) Upanishad

There appears to be some controversy as to the identity
of this Upanishad. There are also a few problems
relating to translation. However, the following reflects
the writings of Deussen and Bloomfield.[1]

This Upanishad consists of three Brahmanas. The first
considers pranava or Om according to its letters. The
second confirms this myth. The third contains thirty-
six questions relating to Om and its answers given by
Prajapati.

First Brahmanam

This asserts that "Brahman created Brahman in a
lotus-flower" a statement that appears self-
contradictory. The "second" Brahman wonders what is
the word by which all desires are obtained.

He practised tapas and saw the two-letter word
having four matras (Om or Aum). He realised that the
first matra 'a' indicated water, acquisition, the earth, fire,
flora, the Rigveda, the Gayatri and Saman, the East, the
spring and a reference to the Self, language, tongue and
speach.

The second matra, u-sound is the atmosphere, wind,
bhuvah, Trishtubh, fifteen-fold Saman, the West,
summer with reference to the self, breath, the nose
and odour.

The third matra 'm' is the sun, heaven, the Samaveda,
svah, the North, the rainy season etc., with reference to
the Self, the light, eyes and vision.

The fouth matra (anusvara) is the water, moon,
Atharvaveda, the South, autumn etc., and with reference
to the self, the heart, the knowledge and the known.

This Om originited before the tapas and is Brahman,
the seed of the Vedas. All mantras have emerged from

Om. When you study the Vedas without tapas, guru, or at a forbidden time, the power of the shruti declines. But with Om which is the essence of the Atharva, this power can be regained. This is the reason why pranava is uttered at the beginning of the sacrificial act and at the end.

If you desire something, observe abstinence for three nights, sleep on straw, sit silently with your face to the East, and mentally chant Om, a thousend times. Your wish will be fulfilled.

Second Brahmanam

Once the city of Indra was besieged by demons (*asuras*). The gods went to Om and praised him and sought his help in defeating the demons. Om helped them but a condition was stipulated. The gods will not study the Vedas before they utter 'Om'. The gods agreed and the asuras were defeated. 'Om' continued to be uttered in all sacred activities and at the beginning of the Vedic studies as agreed.

Third Brahmanam

Prajapati's (P) answers to 34 questions posed by gods (G) are contained in this. We can only mention the important questions and answers.

G- What is the root of Om?

P - The Root is *ap* or 'Ap = Av' indicates surrounding which is like Brahman.

G - What is its pronunciation?

P - It is joint or separate. Both have equal effect.

G - How many matras does it have?

P - They are a, u and m. It is uttered with three reverberations which constitute the half matra.

G - How is it uttered? Can we replace 'm' by nasalisation?

P - With lips. For 'o' the throat is widened, for 'm' the lips are closed. It does not matter if 'm' (*virama*) is changed to nasalisation. It can be uttered in a low, medium or loud tone.

G - What is its colour?

P- White

G- What is its meter?

P- The Gayatri.

G - What is its effect?

P- The path of its effect is that it is uttered at the beginning.

We do not know if this can be interpreted as 'the effect is the same as what you desire in the prayer prefixed by Om.'

In regard to its pronunciation, Prajapati cautions that pranava has been handed down for generations. The best way to learn its pronunciation is to listen to the teacher when he pronounces it. It is better not to ask questions about its pronunciation.

Fifteen

OM IN RITUALS

"In approximate terms Ritual may be defined as a system of acts and sounds, related to each other in accordance with rules *without reference to meaning.*"

—Frits Staal in *Ritual And Mantras: Rules Without Meaning.*

Rituals are not confined to religion; they appear in almost every walk of life. They are a stereotyped or stylised behaviour. Their nature is dependent on social milieu. Rituals may be simple or complex, long or short, flexible or rigid. They make social interaction easy; we know exactly how to behave in a given situation. Manners and etiquettes, election procedure, government formation, military parades, lectures and seminar all have their own rituals.

In religion rites of passage, modes of worship, burial and cremation rites are some examples of rituals.

Meaning and Structure

Basically there are two methods of studying rituals. The first is the most popular and is also the oldest. It has to do with the meaning of rituals and is called the semantic approach. All our discussion in the preceding chapters is related to this method. One of the most important drawbacks of this method is that a ritual or a mantra can be interpreted in several ways. Scholars of religion, sociologists and anthropologists, historians, linguists and psychoanalysts all compete with each other to project their own meaning of a ritual. This gives rise to different 'schools' of interpretation. As time passes every succeeding generation interprets and reinterprets the earlier texts with the result that a ritual can be interpreted, after a few centuries, in hundreds of ways. The manner in which the A-U-M is interpreted is a testimony to multiple interpretations which involves an element of uncertainty.

There is another approach to rituals which is called the syntactic method. In this, we analyse the structures of different rituals and try to find out if there are regular patterns or similarities.

Frits Staal uses this method in his seminal work *Ritual and Mantras: Rules Without Meaning*.

Ritual Structures

All rituals display about ten structures. What is amazing is that music, poetry, dance and a host of other activities which are not classed as ritual behaviour also manifest some or all of these structures. In this chapter, we shall concern ourselves with the structure of mantras and rituals with special reference to Om. You have to remember that structure in this chapter will be considered the primary aspect of rituals, and its meaning, if we discuss, will have only secondary importance.

Rituals in general have the following structures:
1. Iteration (repetition)
2. refrain
3. palindrome (mirror),

4. multiplets
5. embedding
6. relay
7. cycle
8. chorus (concord, unison)
9. pattern completion (structure completion)
10. overlapping. A structure which is characteristic of a ritual containing 'Om' is affixation. Though not independent of the structures mentioned above, it needs to be treated separately.

   1. *Iteration (Repetition)* — In iteration a ritual element is repeated continuously. A japa of Om appears as
      Om Om Om Om ...
      which may be iterated thousands or millions of times.
      Sometimes iteration may appear in which a mantra is repeated and Om is one of its components. For example,
      Hari Om, Hari Om,...
   2. *Refrain* — In verse, refrain is a part of a line or a group of lines which is repeated.
      A ritual element in a hymn may be repeated several times, at the beginning, in the end or in the middle of a line. Consider a part of Shri Ganapati Mantra
      Om Prithviti mantrasya pavitram kuru chasanam Om bhurbhuvah svah Iti asanavidhi 'Atha sanskshepatah kilakam Om Ganeshaya namastubhyam Herambayai kadantine'
      Om is repeated several times as also Ganapati, Ganesha and other names of the god.
   3. *Palindrome* — A palindrome is a word which reads the same from the right to left as from

the left to right. If you walk from pole A to B and back your activity constitutes palindrome. The Common mantras:

(1) Om namah Shivaya, Shivaya namah Om
(2) Om dum Om, are palindromes.

Another palindrome appears in the Yajurveda and Samaveda.

Agnir jyotir jyotir agnir
Indro jyotir jyotir Indrah
Surya jyotir jyotih Suryah

4. *Multiplets* — A multiplet is a group which appears in several mantras and rituals. For example:

Om namah Shivaya
Hari Om
Om tat sat
Bhuh bhuvah svah
Brahma Vishnu Mahesha
Om bhuh bhuvah savah

Most of the above are triplets, one is a duo and one a quartet.

5. *Embedding* — In embedding, a self-sufficient ritual is embedded into a longer ritual. For example, your working in office from 9 A.M. to 5 P.M. is a ritual. If on two days in a week you spend 1 hour each for reading (2 P.M. to 3 P.M.) you are embedding the ritual of reading into the office work.

In religion there are many examples of embedding. For example, achamana is a self-sufficient ritual which appears embedded in other rituals such as sandhya and worship rituals.

Suppose you are doing the japa of *Om namah Shivaya* 1000 times. The japa may be modified in such a way that after every 100 recitations you prostrate before Shiva's idol three times. Prostration is a separate ritual which is embedded in your japa.

6. *Relay* — An activity may be completed by a chain of people. The relay race is an example. In religious rituals relay appears as 'taking over' recitation by one priest from another. Or the priest may ask the *yajamana* to complete the remaining recitation.

7. *Cycle* — In cycle the last ritual element is also the first.
'Om klim hrim Om'
is a cycle.
Similarly,
'Om aim hraum namah roganashan na....
prayanti namah hraum aim Om'
(Saptashati 11-29) is a cycle.

8. *Chorus* — Chorus is a simultaneous performance of the same activity by a number of people.
A bhajana or devotional song is sung by a group of people. Multiplets and invocations such as:
Om namah Shivaya or Om shantih shantih uttered by a group also is an instance of chorus.

9. *Pattern Completion* — This structure arises from our desire to leave a task unfinished. It usually

involves conformity with etiquettes, customs, completion of symmetry, magic numbers and taboos. A few examples will elucidate the point.

You are watching a cricket match. Your favourite batsman makes 98 runs. It is time for you to leave for office. However, you are likely to stay to watch the batsman complete the magic figure of century, though it may entail a mild reprimand from your boss for being late.

You invite a friend for dinner. Though the dinner was believed to be informal, you find that the several courses you offer have made it a formal dinner mentioned in your book of etiquettes. If you serve the guest coffee it will conform to the sequence of courses. You make coffee though your guest is not keen. You have the satisfaction of completing a ritual.

Your child arranges three letter blocks as ABC, BCA. You feel only one combination CAB is left out for the completion of a cycle. You show that combination to your child.

You write "Om gam Ganapati" a number of times. You find that you have actually written it 97 times. You are likely to add three more iterations to reach the figure of 100 before you turn to another task.

To fully appreciate the mechanism of pattern completion, recall the Devanagari alphabet which was considered in chapter 10.

Since we are acquainted with the (Romanized) Sanskrit alphabet, let us nasalise all letters. We get:

am	aam	im	eem	um	oom	*ri*m
*ree*m	*li*m	*lee*m	em	aim	om	aum
kam	kham	gam	gham	ɳam		
cham	chham	jam	jham	n'am		
*ta*m	*th*am	*d*am	*dh*am	*ɳ*am		
tam	tham	dam	dham	nam		
pam	pham	bam	bham	mam		
yam	ram	lam	vam	sham		
*sh*am	sam	ham				

Almost every one of the above nasalized syllables is a bija. This is an example of pattern completion.

Pattern completion is also found in yantras. For example, in asanasiddhi yantra. There is a flower at the centre with eight petals all inscribed with 'Om' displaying symmetry. At the centre is another bija, hreem.

10. *Overlapping* — When a work consists of tasks to be completed by a number of people, there may be overlapping. For example, when mantras are recited by priests in a chain, a priest may start before his predecessor has finished.

11. *Affixation* — A peculiar pattern is present in rituals, which may be called affixation. Certain ritual elements considered important are prefixed, infixed or suffixed. Many bijas and the Gayatri components are used for this purpose. Since Om or pranava is the bija par excellence, it is perhaps the most frequently used word for affixation. Om is also used in combination with other bijas.

Durgasaptashati is a popular text in honour of Goddess Mother, the primordial Power. In saptashati worship a number of bijas are used for prefixing mantras. A few examples involving Om are given below.

(1) For conquering fear — Om sharnagatinarta...
(2) For mesmerizing — Om jnaninamapi...
(3) Removal of poverty — Om Durge...
(4) For wealth — Om sarvabhadha vinirmuktah
(5) Regaining lost prosperity — Om evam...
(6) *Om* may appear in combination with other words. For example,

(1) For destroying fear — Om sharanagat
(2) For mesmerizing — Om jnaninamapi
(3) Removal of poverty — Om Durgesmrita
(4) Eradication of diseases — Om roganashesha

Note that the above combinations are used as prefixes to appropriate mantras to enhance the power of the mantras.

Hundreds of mantras will be found in which Om is used as a prefix and suffix.

1. Om ah namah shivaya ah om (Navakshara mantra)
2. Om dum Om (Durgamantra)
3. Om em hreem sreem namo brahmane dharanam me astvanirakaranam dharayita bhuyasam karnayoh srutam machchydhvam mamayushyam Om (Sri Dharana Sarasvati mantra)
4. Om Rama Om (Rama ekakshara mantra)
   Om when combined with other bijas seem to provide powerful fillers or affixes. Consider a line from Durgamghorastra.
   Om namo em kreem krom sreem hasaum hasfrain hasfrain glaubloom sreem Om bhagavate.....

'Gam' is a bija associated with Ganapati. The combination 'Om gam' affords a powerful tool that can be used for affixation. Shreem is a bija associated with Lakshmi the goddess of wealth. 'Om shreem' is again a compound prefix, suffix or an infix.

We have already considered the Gayatri mantra in connection with Om in detail. We only recall a few instances in which 'Om' is affixed or embedded in the Gayatri or its parts.

1. Om bhuh bhuvah svah Om tatsaviturvarenyam...
2. Om bhurbhuvahsvah Om tatsaviturvarenyam bhargo devasya dhimahi Om dhiyo yo...
3. Om bhuh Om bhuvah Om svah
    Om tatsaviturvarenyam...
    Om dhiyo yo...
4. Om bhuh Om bhuvah Om svah
    Om tatsaviturvarenyam Om bhargo devasya dhimahi
    Om dhiyo...
5. Om bhuh Om bhuvah Om svah Om mahah
    Om janah Om tapah Om satyam Om tatsaviturvarenyam...

See how the Gayatri elements are broken and Om inserted at several places.

Some mantras need to be put under certain samskaras either to activate them or to extricate them from 'curses.'

Bijas like 'soham' and its variants, svadha, Om etc.' are used to energise Vedic and other mantras. For example, the following procedures pertain to Vedic mantras.

1. *Deepanam* hamsa + ishtamantra + soham is a new mantra which is iterated 1000 times.
2. *Abhishekam* Aim hamsa Om, followed by the ishtamantra in turn followed by Aim hamsa Om to be written on a leaf and 'bathed'.

3. *Vimalikaranam* Om traum vashat + ishtamantra + vashat traum Om to be repeated 1000 times.

You will find a number of structures in the above mantras. 1, 2 and 3 are palindromes. 1 and 3 are also iterations of cycles. The ishtamantra is 'embedded' in A,B, C.

Shabar mantras are believed to be cursed by various gods. Their purification is achieved by affixation of certain bijas.

Vimalikaranam — One meditates on the ishtamantra at the muladhara chakra reciting 'Om hraum'.

Deepanam — 'Om hreem sreem' should be prefixed to the ishtamantra.

Only a few samskaras for purifying or energising Vedic and shabar mantras are mentioned here. In fact there can be as many as sixteen rituals needed to make these mantras fit for use.

An interesting example of affixation and 'pattern completion' is found in Meru Tantra:

1. Lam vam are to be prefixed as well as suffixed to the mantra. Every letter of the mantra is nasalised such as am aam kam...
2. Every letter is made 'visarga' such as ah aah kah... etc. These procedures mentioned in Meru Tantra are called awakening of a mantra and should be undertaken only under a guru's instructions.

The syntactic or structural study of mantras and rituals leads to some interesting discoveries. It tells us that most mantras especially bijas are not language. Frits Staal has gone further and posited that at least some Vedic rituals and mantras are devoid of meaning. We shall discuss more about this aspect with special reference to Om, in chapter 16.

Sixteen

LANGUAGE AND PSYCHOLOGY

"Religion is opium for the masses."

—Karl Marx

In chapters 1 through 14 we discussed the status of Om from the religious view point. In the previous chapter the approach was non-religious but syntactic. In this chapter we shall briefly discuss the secular but semantic approach i.e., how the scholars of linguistics and psychology interpret Om.

Many scholars have asked themselves whether mantras are language. When we examine the bijas like Om, hrim, am or stobhas like ha, bu, etc., we notice two prominent characteristics. They are not listed in ordinary dictionaries. Though every bija is assigned a meaning, the bija is used more like a magical utterance than a linguistic piece. We have also seen that Om, for example, may be used with any frequency.

It is believed that animals too utter similar sounds. We notice regular patterns in mewing, neighing, bleating, cackling, grunting and chirping. Bird songs have been investigated in depth and it is found that like rituals described in chapter 15, they display similar structural characteristics. This has led many scholars of religion to postulate that some mantras show patterns rather than meaning. These mantras especially bijas like Om, am, aam, antedate language i.e., they were present before humankind began to speak. They are in fact, the remnants of what we uttered during our evolution.

Linguistic expressions do not obey ritual patterns mentioned in chapter 15.

If you hear someone chant "Om Om Om Om Om hail to Shiva," you will not be surprised but if someone says "I I I I I worship God" you are likely to doubt the sanity of the worshipper. Similarly "Om Om Rama Om Om" would be accepted as a normal prayer, but a linguistic piece like "I I I hate you you" would evoke laughter.

We mentioned relay and chorus as two of the patterns in rituals and mantras. In ordinary language we do not find this pattern. If a boss asks a team consisting of A, B, C, whether the project entrusted to them is complete, we would hardly expect the following reply :

A- We have completed 30% of

B - the work. We need

C- additional funds immediately.

Or

A, B, C in unison - We have completed 30% of the work. We need additional funds immediately.

We also mentioned in the previous chapter that palindrome is a pattern mantras display. However, an expression like, say:

"I am going to dance to going am I", will not be found in language, except perhaps in the utterances of a circus buffoon.

It is surmised, therefore, that since mantras do not obey the linguistic rules and bija-like sounds are uttered by animals, mantras antedate language.

Some scholars like Frits Staal even go further and assert that some types of mantras and ritual (for example, those related to srauta ritual) have no meaning.

Another aspect that distinguishes mantras from language is manifest when a literary work including mantras is 'exported' i.e., translated in other languages. It is found, that while ordinary linguistic expressions are translated, the mantras are transliterated. This is especially so in case of bijas and stobhas which even to us appear meaningless, and which could have been born before language come into existence. Transliteration is, of course, subject to adaptation, a process in which a new word is absorbed with phonetic modifications suitable to the new environment. For example, 'homa' in Sanskrit becomes 'goma' in Japanese.

Om vajra karma kam

(Om thunderbolt rite)

in Japanse becomes

Om bazaar kyarna ken

In Sanskrit "Om bhuh kham" means "Om earth, space". In Japanese it becomes "Om boku ken". All these words are adapted transliterations.

It is necessary to remember that the mantras like Om, kleem, hreem do not decline. This is in contrast to the grammatical rules in Sanskrit in which declensions abound. This makes a strong case in favour of those who maintain that at least some types of mantras are not language.

Vinoba Bhave in his book *The Study of Upanishads* contends that Om has the same etymology as *omni* which means 'all' or 'everything'. A Latin root, 'omni' is used in many compound words in English and many European languages (omnipresent, omnivorous, omniscient etc.).

If you go through an English dictionary you will find a number of such words. However, if you inspect a Sanskrit dictionary, you will not find any compound word derived from a root comparable with 'omni'. It seems that the resemblance between Om and omni has an origin which has to do with the human vocal apparatus and the ease with which certain bija-like words can be uttered. Bhave's contention that Om and 'omni' are semantically connected does not seem to be endorsed by linguists.

Baby's Utterances

Many scholars such as Roman Jakobson and Morris Hall have studied the utterances of human babies in depth. According to them the most natural order of sound production is an opening of the mouth followed by its closure. It would, therefore, be easy to explain why the sounds like Om, am, im, hum are uttered universally by all human babies.

After this babbling stage the baby enters the "consonant plus vowel" stage when mama, papa, baba appear natural pronunciation. It would surprise you to know that there is considerable resemblance between the easiest words spoken in different languages. Most of these words are associated with the objects with which the baby comes into contact. The meaning of words may differ in different languages but there is no doubt that these monosyllabic and bisyllabic words originated in the baby's utterings. A few examples will elucidate the point.

The following 'words' are some of the easiest utterances, a human baby can make.

Aba, abba, abu, amma, anna, am, im, Om, um, ona
Baba baby, bhubhu
Ma, mom, mama, mami, mamma, miau
Papa, phupha, phuphi, pop
Some of these are apparently meaningless phonemes like im, Om, um, ona while some have meaning. For example *mama* can mean mother in many Indo-European languages but can also mean maternal uncle in some Indian languages. Usually when such monosyllables and bisyllables have meaning, they indicate an object with which the baby comes into contact at the earliest stages. For example, abu, abba indicate 'father' in semitic languages while 'amma' means mother or lady in some Indian languages. What is interesting is that the baby utters these phonemes before she is taught what they mean.

Many psychologists have been influenced by Haeckel's biogenic law according to which the development of the individual organism or *ontogeny* recapitulates or mimics the development of the species or *phylogeny*. It would appear, therefore, that the human baby's babbling which resembles bijas and stobhas like Om, um, hum bababa, gogo etc., are remnants of what our distant ancestors uttered during evolution.

There is another field which indicates the genesis of bijas. It is abnormal psychology. According to the Freudian theory the abnormal behaviour of the emotionally disturbed patients reflects the fixation at an earlier stage of the person. With the application of the Haeckel's law it would appear that the abnormal ritual-like behaviour which includes repeated mantra like - utterances should be ascribed to the pre-linguistic stage.

Some scholars believe that mantras not only antedate language but "language derived from mantras in course of evolution."[1] Staal presents a tentative hypothesis in which he perceives three stages of evolution.

In the first stage are mantras of Type I. These are the sounds which are subject to phonological constraints. The bijas like hum, him, em, Om or stobhas such as bham would fall into this category. Staal believes that the first stage exemplifies the sounds found among vertebrates which existed in the pre-human stage.

In the second stage, the mantras of type II appeared. These were extensions of type I, more complex and sometimes subject to syntactic constraints. They appeared like sequences of Type I : For example ha bu ha bu ha bu .... or

Om am aam ....

In the third or final stage the mantras acquired semantic feature and became syntactically more complex. He believes that the second stage may be anthropoid or features of early humans. The final stage, he guesses, covers about fifty to hundred thousand years during which our language developed.

We need not comment on this speculation, but the above discussion will convince you that a strong probability exists in favour of the theory that Om, like other bijas am, hum, etc. have roots in the baby's utterings.

We leave it to scholars to decide why Om became a sacred symbol and was interpreted as AUM consisting of three and and a half matras (moras).

Psychology

In chapter 15 we discussed the role of Om in rituals. We confined ourselves to the structural approach to rituals. Since Om plays a significant role in rituals and can be called a ritual mantra, it would be worthwhile to consider the semantic approach too — what psychologists, sociologists and anthropologists have to say about rituals.

In regard to the general rituals, which reflect our stylised behaviour, it is not difficult to conjecture their utility. Rituals make social interaction easy. We know exactly how to behave in a given situation.

However, more academic explanations may also be offered. Those who call themselves existentialists believe that our anxiety is rooted in our very existence. It may, therefore, be contended that certainty and determinacy inherent in ritual behaviour reduces our existential anxiety. Without rituals we would perpetually face the dread of uncertainty.

Transactional Analysis (TA) too offers insights into the genesis of social rituals. According to TA every infant needs to be stimulated. Apart from the 'stimulation hunger', TA also recognizes structure - hunger; the problem of how to structure our time when we are awake. As the child grows, the stimulation hunger is converted into recognition hunger. All of us know that we feel neglected when we are invited to a function and we find that no one takes cognizance of our presence. According to TA social rituals play the role of satiating these hungers. In their jargon 'stroke' is a fundamental unit of social action. So important are strokes - greeting, patting, acknowledging our presence, praising in our life that a 'no - stroke' is considered worse than a mild punitive stroke in the development of a child.

Zoologists have also studied animal rituals which seem to have many similarities — especially repetition — with human rituals. A primate who is isolated and deprived of normal rituals shows the same kind of anxiety and depression as an isolated human being would display.

Clinical psychologists mention several ego 'defences' which we display when we have excessive anxiety and guilt. These defences serve to protect our ego which is under threat.

Some of these defences may be briefly described. *Denial of reality* is a defence displayed by most of us in stress : we may ignore the threat, we may mitigate the inevitable death by postulating the glorious world after death. Closely related to this shield is *fantasy* in which a poor person may day-dream of becoming rich overnight, or a coward may believe that he would be a hero once he finds the right key — say a mantra or a ritual.

In *rationalization* we resort to the mode of thinking which would justify our anti-social behaviour or which would mitigate our failure. In *projection* we attribute to others our own unacceptable tendencies : usually this helps us shift the blame to others. *Repression* is a defence which makes our painful experience or harmful desires unconscious. We selectively forget what we do not want to remember, but the forgotten matter is subject to our unconscious forces. In *reaction formation* a person not only represses undesirable material but unconsciously develops opposite behaviour patterns. This is usually found among the guardians of public morality, and perpetual preachers.

Undoing or *atonement* is perhaps the most important defence for our purpose. Since we have been taught in childhood that a sin is punished we develop many mechanisms to atone for our perceived wrong doings. A person who feels guilty may go on a donation spree. He may indulge in such acts as washing hands, cleaning or repeating the same magical word.

These activities are perceived to be cleansing agents.

In *regression* the anxiety-driven person goes back to earlier stages of development and may display infantile behaviour. It is possible to regard utterance of Om as a sign of regression to the infantile stage when the baby uttered Om and similar bija-like monosyllables.

Displacement is a defence in which there is a shift of emotion, memories, symbolic meanings etc., so that a trauma becomes less painful. In *emotional insulation* and *intellectualization* we try to pooh-pooh the intensity of the threat or may indulge in pseudologic as a counter to our emotional pain or guilt. Many cynics hide their insecurity behind the facade of intellectualisation of an emotional situation.

Sublimation is the word used to indicate the manner in which a person channels his or her instinctual — especially sexual — energy in socially acceptable expressions and goals. For example, a woman not able to marry may become a dedicated nurse or social worker. However, many psychologists and sociologists doubt that a frustrated sexual drive can be entirely sublimated.

All of us, whether we are normal or clinically abnormal, use not one but a number of defences simultaneously to reduce our anxiety.

In religion, rituals and mantras play the role of reducing the anxiety and guilt of those who perform them. The very word 'mantra' implies that it is a protecting device.

Recitation of sacred mantras repeatedly is believed to have an effect in proportion to the length for which the mantra is repeated. Om, the Gayatri and even simple mantras like 'Rama, Rama' are perceived to reduce our anxiety and wash our sins.

Clinical psychologists and psychiatrists find their patients using an arsenal of various defences to protect their ego. Psychoanalyst A. P. Sidhar cites the case of a borderline paranoid "who would utter Om at the slightest opportunity as a defence against fantasies of external attacks by those plotting to destroy him and (Om) was an immediate effective means for him to feel strong and be able to control and eliminate his persecutors with the powers derived from the recitation of Om."

It must be remembered that while Om acts as a defence shield, the paranoid state in which the individual feels that he is being persecuted, plotted against, maltreated or ignored by his 'enemies', sometimes the whole world, itself is a conjuction of many defences. The most important defence is *projection*. When a person who harbours inferiority feelings and feels insecure, he cannot accept his failure or frustration. Instead of owning the blame and accepting his weak points he uses projection to blame his 'enemies' for his plight.

It would be pertinent to mention here what are termed erotogenic or erogenous zones which are those parts of the body which give rise to sexual feeling when stimulated. They include lips, breasts and sexual organs. Sigmund Freud observes in his *A General*

Introduction to Psychoanalysis: "Sucking for nourishment becomes the point of departure from which the whole sexual life develops, the unattainable prototype of every later sexual satisfaction, to which in times of need phantasy often enough reverts."[2] These words indicate that according to Freud, feeding creates a permanent bond between the breast and the infant which lasts even when the child becomes an adult.

Sidhar compares this primordial sound (Om) with the first sound which emerges from the new-born human baby and also when the baby is sucking the breast. These sounds do have considerable resemblance with Om. According to him, it becomes "the word-symbol for the mother into which the infant can project all emotions — pleasures and pains." The child associates Om or Aum with mother, omnipotence and the nourishing breast. Throughout his life, whenever he feels threatened, he goes back to Om, the nourishing mother which gives him succour.

Sidhar has developed his theory further, but its nature is too technical to be discussed here.

It is interesting to see how several defences are brought into play in connection with ritualisation of Om. First, there is regression to the feeding stage in search of security. Repression enables one to jettison the guilt attached to the sexual component of breast feeding. Using displacement and attempted sublimation, Om is elevated to the divine level, so that the guilt is further reduced. Mother is also sometimes worshipped as Mother Goddess in the process.

However, these attempts to cut off the guilt are not always successful. One part of the worshipper's mind is conscious of reality. In order to perpetuate the fantasy he has created, he may have to resort to continual ritualisation of Om.

NOTES

2. The Vedas and Brahman

1. See Tigunait (1983), Chapter 7 for a detailed discussion on the theory of sound. Woodroffe also discusses mantras and sound in Chapter 4.

3. Upanishads (I)

1. Quoted by Sarvananda in *Taittiriyopanishad* page 43.
2. Quoted by Sarvananda in *Taittiriyopanishad* pp 61-62.

6. Ganesha

1. As mentioned earlier there is no unanimity among scholars on the objects Ganesha holds in his hands. The original Sanskrit poem by Deshpande will be found in Athavale (1996) p. 196.

10. Mantras and Mantrashastra

1. Strictly speaking, t, th, d, dh, n are labo-dental sounds in which the tip of the tongue presses against the teeth, and are closer to the sounds in French or Spanish. However, those who are not familiar with these sounds may pronounce them as in English.

14. Yoga, Gods and Pranava

1. It may interest you to know that the Upanishads became known to Europe for the first time through

the Persian-Latin translation of *Oupnek'hat* which in turn is a Persian translation of 50 Upanishads. The Pronou (Pranava) Upanishad, presented here heavily relies on this source.

16. Language and Psychology

1. Staal, p. 265
2. Freud, p.323

GLOSSARY

A

Adibija - "First seed", Om.

Advaita - Non-dualism, a Vedantic school of philosophy.

Agni - Fire treated as god.

Ahavania - The third of the three sacrificial fires, associated with 'm' of Aum.

Akasha - "Space" or "ether", one of the five material constituents of the universe.

Ananda-Bliss.

Antahkarana - Collectively, manas (mind) buddhi (intellect), chitta (pleasure-seeking faculty) and ahankara (ego).

Anumana - Inference.

Ap - Water, the second element constituting the universe.

Apana - The vital energy (prana) which carries unassimilated food downwards.

Aranyaka- One of the sections of the Vedas.

Asana - "posture"; the third stage in Patanjali yoga.

Ashtanga yoga - The yoga of "eight limbs", Patanjali yoga.

Atman - The self identified with Brahman or the Supreme Soul in advaita philosophy.

Atmajnana - Knowledge of Atman.

AUM - Om, letters A, U, M have been interpreted in several ways. See Appendix.

Avidya - Ignorance in Vedantic philosophy.

Avighnesha - The remover of obstacles, Lord Ganesha.

B

Bagalamukhi - A tantric path relating to one of the ten great goddesses; the queen of forbidden tantra.

Bija (beeja) mantra - 'Seed' mantra usually monosyllabic but can consist of upto ten syllables. According to tantra, para bindu whose substance is Supreme Shakti splits into three parts - bindu, nada and bija.

Bhuh, bhuvah, svah - 'earth, sky, heaven', vyahritis prefixed to the Gayatri mantra.

Bindu - 'Dot'. In tantra and yoga it can mean liquor, sexual energy, concentrated energy at or above the ajna chakra. See also Bija mantra.

Brahma - The creator God, the first of the trinity, the others are Vishnu, Shiva.

Brahmacharya - Celibacy, also practice leading to liberation.

Brahman - The Ultimate Reality in Vedanta.

Brahmana - One of the two main sections of the Vedas.

Brahmananda - Supreme Bliss.

Brahma-sutras - A treatise on Vedanta philosophy attributed to Vyasa.

Buddha - 'The enlightened one', specifically Gautama the founder of Buddhism.

C

Chakra - 'Wheel'. The point where more than three energy channels (nadis) meet. The major chakras are along the spinal cord. Also refers to yantra and mandala.

Chakra puja - Worship of chakras usually referring to the left-hand Kaula practice.

D

Dakshina - The second of the three sacrificial fires, associated with 'u' of Aum.

Darshana - 'Glimpse', system of philosophy.

Devas - 'shining ones'; the gods of Hindu mythology.

Dharana - 'Concentration', sixth step of Patanjali yoga.

Dharma - Righteousness, duty.

Dhyana - Meditation, One-pointed concentration, seventh stage of Patanjali yoga.

Divine Mother - The highest ferminine aspect of the deity worshipped in tantra as Shakti (power). It has different manifestations : Bagalmukhi, Bhuvaneshvari, Chhinamasta, Dhumavati, Kamala, Kali, Matangi, Tripura (Sri Vidya), Tara, Tripura Bhairavi; also collectively called Maha Vidya or 'Great knowledge'.

E

Ekadanta - 'Having one tusk', Ganesha.

F

Freud — Sigmund (1856-1939) — Founder of psycho-analysis.

G

Ganesha - Elephant-headed god. Also called Gajanana, Gaja- vadana, Kari-mukha, Heramba ("boastful"), Lamba-karna (long-eared), Lambodara (pendant-bellied), Dri-deha (double bodied), Vighna-harta (remover of obstacles).

Ganesha Gita - The Bhagvad-Gita in which the name of Krishna is replaced by that of Ganesha. Used by Ganapateyas or the worshippers of Ganesha.

Ganesha Purana - An Upa-Purana describing the glories of Ganesha.

Gaudapada - Author of *Karika*, a commentary on the Mandukya Upanishad.

Garhapatya - The first of the three sacrificial fires, associated with 'a' of Aum.

Gayatri - A most sacred mantra in the Rigveda addressed to the sun. Personified as goddess Savitri. Also a Vedic meter.

Guna - (Sankhya philosophy) one of the three qualities; sattva (righteousness), rajas (activity), tamas (dullness), attributed to Prakriti (Nature or matter).

Guru - Spiritual teacher.

H

Hiranya Garbha - 'Golden egg' or 'golden womb' In the Rigveda it is stated to have arisen in the beginning; lord of all things.

Hridaya - 'Heart'. In tantra it means that aspect of mantra which is to be visualized, synchronized or "deposited" on the heart center. Also a sadhana involving recitation of mantras, which enables the worshipper to identify himself with the power of mantra.

I

Indra - The king of Vedic gods, also the god of weather.

Ishta Deva - A personal form of Brahman; also a personal manifestation of a mantra.

Ishvara - The Personal God, corresponds to saguna Brahman i.e., Brahman with attributes.

J

Jaimini (ca 200 BCE) - A disciple of Vyasa and the founder of the Purva Mimamsa philosophy.

Japa - Repetition of a mantra.

Jiva - 'Living being'. Individual soul.

Jivanamukti - 'Liberation' during one's own life time.

Jnana - knowledge, knowledge of Truth.

K

Krishna - 'Black'. Vishnu's incarnation who related the *Bhagavad Gita* to Arjuna on the battlefield, and acted as his charioteer.

Kundali - 'Coil' or 'bangle', see Kundalini Shakti.

Kundalini Shakti - The energy dormant in the muladhara chakra which is awakened by yogic methods; also called Kundalini Devi. Believed to be coiled when dormant.

M

Madhva (1199-1276 CE) - Founder of Dualistic school of Vedanta philosophy.

Mahah - A vyahriti sometimes identified with Brahman.

Maha Vidya - See Divine Mother.

Manas - The faculty of volition and doubt, mind.

Mantras - The sacred formula used in japa. Also one of the two sections of the Vedas.

Manu - The law-giver of ancient India author of *Manusamhita*.

Maya - The cosmic illusion due to which *one* appears as *many*. Ignorance preventing an individual to see the One or Brahman.

Modaka - A cookie, Ganesha's favourite.

Moksha - Liberation, freedom from the cycle of birth and death.

Mudra - "Seal" Hand gestures used in yoga, tantra and some forms of worship.

Muni - A holy sage.

N

Nirvana - 'Blowing out'; annihilation of ego, passion and desire; liberation.

Nrisimha (Narasimha) - Vishnu's incarnation as man-lion.

Nyasa - A technique according to which elements of mantras are 'deposited' on different parts of the body.

Nyaya - One of the orthodox schools of Indian philosophies, founded by Gautam. It is mainly concerned with methodology and logic.

O

Om (Aum) - Pranava, primordial sound also called adibija, Udgitha; identified with Brahman.

P

Para - 'Transcendent'. The highest state of vak (sound) according to Mimamsa philosophy.

Patanjali (2nd century BCE) - The author of the Yoga Sutras and the founder of Yoga philosophy.

Prajna - Consciousness in the dreamless sleep.

Prakriti - Primordial Nature with gunas.

Prana - Life-force having modifications; also the first modification which controls the breath. Also a name of the active Cosmic Soul.

Pranava - Om.

Prithvi - Earth, the fifth constituent of the universe.

Puranas - Books of Hindu mythology.

Purusha - 'Person'. In Samkhya philosophy it indicates the conscious principle.In Vedanta it also connotes the soul and the Absolute.

R

Rama - Incarnation of Vishnu and the hero of *Ramayana*.

Ramakrishna (1836 - 1886) - A great saint and mystic.

Ramanuja (1017-1137 CE) - Philosopher - saint, the founder of qualified non-dualism.

Rishi - A seer of truth.

S

Sadhana - 'Accomplishing', spiritual practice.

Samadhi - Trance-like state, communion with God.

Samana - The vital energy (prana) which carries nutrition all over the body.

Samaya - 'One with her'. A meditative school of tantra.

Sanatana dharma - 'Eternal religion', refers to Vedic religion.

Sanyasa - Monastic life.

Shakti - Power, treated as Mother Goddess in tantra.

Shanti - 'Peace', but can mean inaction, lack of response, indifference etc, also interpreted as Brahman.

Shiva - Father of Ganesha.

Shruti - The Vedas.

Sri Chakra - The chakra of the Divine Mother also called Sri Yantra.

Sri Mata - Divine Mother.

Sri Vidya - 'Auspicious knowledge' The most important of the ten Maha Vidyas; also Divine Mother.

Sri Yantra - Sri Chakra.

Stobhas - Meaningless syllables found in the Samaveda. They are similar to bijas.

Sushumna - The central energy channel that runs along the spinal column from its base to the crown of the head.

T

Taijasa - Conscionsness in the dream state.

Tapas - 'That which generates heat'. Austerity, spiritual discipline.

Turiya - 'The fourth'. Brahman which both pervades and transcends three states of waking, dream and deep sleep.

U

Udana - The vital energy (prana) which ejects the contents of the stomach through the mouth.

Udgata (Udgatri) - The priest who chants Sama verses.

Udgitha - One of the five or seven parts of the Samaveda; also Om.

Upasana - 'Sitting near', worship.

V

Vahana - 'Vehicle' used by gods. Ganesha's vahana is a rat.

Vaishvanara - Conscionsness in the waking state. Also called Vaishvanarah, Vishvanara or simply Vishva.

Vashistha - A rishi and Rama's master. He consoled Rama when he was disgusted with life. His preaching appears in the text *Yoga Vashistha.*

Vayu - Air, treated as a god in the Vedas.

Vedanta - 'The conclusion of the Vedas'. A system of philosophy attributed to Vyasa, elaborated in Upanishads, Bhagvad Gita and Brahma-sutras.

Videhamukti - 'Liberation' after death. A *Videhamukta* is not reborn.

Vighnaharta - Remover of obstacles, Ganesha.

Vishishtadvaita - Qualified non-dualism according to

which individual souls and the universe are parts of Brahman. Founded by Ramanuja, it is one of the schools of Vedanta.

Vyahriti - 'Covering'. The first three vyahritis are *bhuh, bhuvah, svah* usually prefixed to the Gayatri mantra. The other four are *mahah, janah, tapah, satyam.*

Vyana - The vital energy (prana) pervading the whole body.

Y

Yajnavalkya - An ancient sage to whom is attributed the White (Shukla) Yajurveda, the Shathapata Brahmana, the Brihad Aranyaka and Yajnavalkyasmriti.

Yama - God of death.

Yantra - "Device" A geometric figure usually with inscriptions, used in worship especially in tantra.

Yoga - Union of the individual soul with the Supreme Soul. Any method leading to such union. A path of liberation. Specifically, Patanjali's Yoga system of darshana.

BIBLIOGRAPHY

Acharya, S. S. (2001). *Rig Veda Vol. I – IV*. Sanskriti Sansthan, Bareli.

(1998). *Sama Veda*. Sanskriti Sansthan, Bareli.

(2001). *Yajur Veda*. Sanskriti Sansthan, Bareli.

(1998). *Atharva Veda Vol. I – II*. Sanskriti Sansthan, Bareli.

Athavale, Shantaram (1996). *Omkara Rahasya*. Anjali, Pune.

Bapat, K. M. (-). *Gorakshanath Yoga*. Raghuvanshi Prakashan, Pune.

Basham, A. L. (2001). *The Wonder That Was India*. Rupa & Co., New Delhi.

Berne, Eric (1968). *Games People Play*. Penguin, Middlesex.

Bhave, Vinoba (1999). *Upanishadancha Abhyas*. Paramdham Prakashan, Pravanar.

Bose, A.C. (1970). *The Call Of The Vedas*. Bharatiya Vidya Bhavan, Mumbai.

Burde, Jayant (2004). *Rituals, Mantras and Science : An Integral Perspective*.Motilal Banarasidass, Delhi.

Chakravarti, Mohan (2000). *Indrajal*. Kshirasagar and Co., Pune.

Chidbhavananda, Swami (1965). *The Bhagavad Gita*. Sri Ramakrishna Tapovanan, Tirupparaitturai.

Desai, C. G. (2002). *Gayatri Mantra Sadhana*. Manorama Prakashan, Mumbai.

Deussen, Paul (1980). *Sixty Upanishads of the Veda, Vol. II*. Motilal Banarasidass, Delhi.

Frazer, James (1993). *The Golden Bough.* Wordsworth Editions, Hertfordshire.

Freud, Sigmund (1960). *A General Introduction to Psychoanalysis.* Washington Square,N.Y.

Gambhirananda, Swami (1989). *Mandukya Upanishad.* Advaita Ashram, Calcutta.

Ghaisas, D. A. (2003). *Bhavartha Jnaneshvari.* Manorama Prakashan, Mumbai.

Hockett, Charles F. (1958). *A Course in Modern Linguistics.* Oxford & IBH, New Delhi.

Iyengar, B. K. S. (1992). *Light on Yoga.* Harper Collins, New Delhi.

Morris, Desmond (1984). *The Naked Ape.* Laurel, N. Y. (1994). *The Human Zoo.* Vintage, London.

O' Flaherty, Wendy Doniger (2000). *The Rig Veda.* Penguin, New Delhi.

Rama, Swami (1998). *Meditation and its Practice.* The Himalayan Institute Press, Honesdale.

Sarvananda, Swami (-). *Aitareyopanisad.* Sri Ramakrishna Math, Madras.

(-). *Prasna Upanisad.* Sri Ramakrishna Math, Madras.

(-). *Taittiriyopanisad.* Sri Ramakrishna Math, Madras.

Sasine, Jayvijay (1999). *Kundalinichya Shodhat.* Vedanta Publishers, Mumbai.

Sankaracarya, Adi (1978). *Atmabodha.* Sri Ramakrisna Math, Madras.

(1975). *Bhaja Govindam.* Sri Ramakrisna Math, Madras.

Sankaracarya (108), Sriyogesvaranandatirtha (1996). *Mantrashastra.* Keshav Bhikaji Dhavale, Mumbai.

Sidhar, A.P. (2004). *OM - The Mystic Symbol, A Psychoanalytic View.* (Unpublished paper)

Staal, Frits (1996). *Ritual and Mantras: Rules Without Meaning.* Motilal Banarasidass, Delhi.

Svanandasarasvati (-). *Patanjala Yogavidya.* Raghuvanshi Prakashan, Pune.

Swami Ashokananda (1995). *Avadhuta Gita of Dattatreya.* Sri Ramakrishna Math, Madras.

Swahananda, Swami (1956). *Chandogya Upanishad,* Sri Ramakrishna Math, Madras.

Tigunait, Pandit Rajmani (1983). *Seven Systems of Indian Philosophy.* The Himalayan International Institute of Yoga science and philosophy of the U. S. A., Honesdale.

(1996). *The Power of Mantra & The Mystery of Initiation.* The Himalayan International Institute of Yoga science and philosophy of the U. S. A., Honesdale. (1999). *Tantra Unveiled.* The Himalayan International Institute of Yoga science and Philosophy of the U. S. A., Honesdale.

Tyagisananda, Swami (-). *Svetasvatara Upanishad.* Sri Ramakrishana Math, Madras.

Unmeshanand (1997). *Shastra Ase Sangate Part I.* Vedwani Prakashan, Kolhapur.

(1999). *Shastra Ase Sangate Part II.* Vedwani Prakashan, Kolhapur.

(1997). *Tumche Pourohitya Tumhich Kara, Part I.* Vedwani Prakashan, Kolhapur.

(2000). *Tumche Pourohitya Tumhich Kara, Part II.* Vedwani Prakashan, Kolhapur.

Woodroffe, John (1997). *The Serpent Power.* Ganesha & Co., Madras.

APPENDIX

Interpretations of AUM

A	U	M	Source
Agni	Vayu	Indra	Isha, Kena Upanishads
Rigveda	Yajurveda	Samaveda	Brihad Aranyaka Upanishad
Earth	Sky	Heaven	Brihad Aranyaka Upanishad
Speech	Manas	Prana	Brihad Aranyaka Upanishad
Humankind	Manes	Gods	Brihad Aranyaka Upanishad
Mother's Instruction	Father's instruction	Guru's instruction	Brihad Aranyaka Upanishad
Jnana yoga	Karma yoga	Bhakti yoga	Bhagavad Gita
Tamas (guna)	Rajas	Sattva	Bhagavad Gita
Yajna	Donation	Austerity	Bhagavad Gita
'Tajja'	'Talla'	'Tadan'	Chhandogya Upanishad
Ut	Gih	Tham	Chhandogya Upanishad
Sthula deha	Sukshma deha	Karana deha	Mandukya Upanishad
Vaishvanara	Taijas	Prajna	Mandukya Upanishad
Waking	Dream	Dreamless sleep	Mandukya Upanishad
Past	Present	Future	Mandukya Upanishad
Shiva's first eye	Second eye	Third eye	Rigveda
Para	Pashyanti	Madhyama	Rigveda
Lakshmi	Shakti	Sarasvati	Rigveda
Asana	Pranayama	Pratyahara	Yogasutra
Dharana	Dhyana	Samadhi	Yogasutra
What	How much	How	Kathopanishad
Prana	Apana	Vyana	Taittiriya Upanishad

INDEX

BOOKS OF RELATED INTEREST

ANCIENT
Teachings for Spiritual
Growth

Douglas De Long

ISBN: 81-87967-68-4

**ART AS A GUIDE TO
SELF-REALIZATION**

J. Donald Walters

81-7822-028-8

**COME, COME, YET
AGAIN COME**

Osho

81-7822-154-3

COMING HOME
The Experience of
Enlightenment in
Sacred Traditions

Lex Hixon

81-7822-158-6

**DIET FOR
TRANSCENDENCE**
Vegetarianism and the
World Religions

Steven Rosen

81-7822-201-9

**DANCING WITH
THE VOID**
The Innerstandings of a
Rare-born Mystic

Sunyata

81-7822-134-9

**DISCOVERING THE
REALM BEYOND
APPEARANCE**
Pointers to the
Inexpressible

Robert Powell

81-7822-130-6

**EASTERN
SPIRITUALITY FOR
MODERN LIFE**
Exploring Buddhism,
Hinduism, Taoism and
Tantra

David Pond

81-7822-199-3

**ECOLOGICAL
SPIRITUALITY**
Hindu Scriptural
Perspectives

G. Naganathan

81-7822-182-9

NOBODY HOME
From Belief to Clarity

Jan Kersschot

81-7822-192-6

INTUITIVE LIVING
A Sacred Path

Alan Seale

81-7822-098-9

KARMIC FACTS & FALLACIES

Ina Marx

81-7822-069-5

LIVING ENLIGHTENMENT
A Call for Evolution Beyond Ego

Andrew Cohen

81-7822-142-x

REBELLION REVOLUTION & RELIGIOUSNESS

Osho

81-7822-149-7

PATH WITHOUT FORM
A Journey into the Realm Beyond Thought

Robert Powell

81-7822-135-7

HIMALAYAN MYSTICISM
Shiva's Disc to cut Asunder and Open the Mystic Heart

Ralph Nataraj

81-7822-290-6

SATISFYING OUR INNATE DESIRE
How We Can Be Spiritually Awake and Live as the Divine Beings We Really Are

Roy Eugene Davis

81-7822-198-5

LIVING INTIMATELY
A Guide to Realizing Spiritual Unity in Relationships

Judith Blackstone

81-7822-143-8